How to Turn Around a Financially Troubled Company

H. Ronald Kibel

McGraw-Hill Book Company

New York St. Louis San Francisco Auckland
Bogotá Hamburg Johannesburg London Madrid
Mexico Montreal New Delhi Panama Paris
São Paulo Singapore Sydney Tokyo Toronto

Library of Congress Cataloging in Publication Data

Kibel, H. Ronald (Harvey Ronald)
How to turn around a financially troubled company.

Includes index.
1. Corporations—Finance.   I. Title.
HC4026.K46   658.1′5   81-23656
AACR2

1234567890   D O D O   898765432

ISBN 0-07-034540-6

The editors for this book were Olive Collen and Jon Palace, the designer was Jules Perlmutter, and the production supervisor was Sally Fliess.
It was set in Electra by University Graphics, Inc. Printed and bound by R. R. Donnelly & Sons Company.

To Isabel, Ellen, and Paul

About the Author

H. Ronald Kibel has been the confidential, behind-the-scenes adviser to many top executives and owners of troubled companies.

He was a prominent business executive and was in charge of the Los Angeles General Consulting Practice for Peat, Marwick, Mitchell & Co., one of the world's largest international professional firms. He has lectured extensively and taught at the University of Southern California Graduate School.

He is currently chairman of the board of the American Cancer Society in California and is an officer in the Young President's Organization.

He received his B.S. in Industrial Engineering from Columbia University, where he graduated with top honors, and his M.S. from the University of Southern California, where he graduated at the top of his class.

His background is unique because he has been "on the hot seat" and advised those executives in the same position. The material for this book comes from his experiences. Exhibits are modified to protect client confidentiality.

He resides in the Brentwood area of Southern California with his wife, Isabel (a fiber artist), and two children, Ellen and Paul.

Contents

Preface

I have always believed that a need existed for a "hands-on" book to assist troubled executives and professionals during their time of need. Further, I believe the executives and professionals of healthy companies can do much to protect their position.

The idea for this book came as a natural consequence of observing that companies heading toward a crisis and those in the crisis exhibit common characteristics. More important was the observation that the approaches toward solving the crisis were similar for companies in varying types of businesses.

My concentrated involvement with many turnaround situations over my career has afforded me a wealth of background material. The difficult task was to evaluate, analyze, synthesize, prioritize, and summarize my own experience in a form useful to the reader.

I could not have embarked on this task without the patience of my wife Isabel and the advice and assistance received from many quarters. In particular, I would like to thank Mr. Robert Shutan, partner in the law firm of Sidley and Austin, specializing in bankruptcy work, for his guidance; and Ms. Sheila Hutman, for her superb initial editing of my first work.

Without them and many others too numerous to mention, this book would not have been possible.

H. Ronald Kibel

Chapter 1

Introduction

Everything seems to fall apart when your company finds itself in trouble. Trusted advisers—attorneys, accountants, and consultants—run for cover, pointing their trembling index fingers at those key executives who failed to heed their sage advice. Past supporters—banks and financial institutions, stockholders, and vendors—are suddenly less cordial. The kind, understanding bank executive with whom you occasionally lunched (and who may have even paid the bill) is replaced by an older, hardened, usually bald-headed man. This person threatens to call in your loan, reduce your level of credit, and take over your home and all you own as collateral; at any moment, he will ask for your children as. hostages. Once-friendly shareholders, who last year claimed you were the genius of the financial world, are now questioning your leadership, your sanity, and, at times, your honesty. Those wonderful vendors, who often treated you and your staff to fantastic gourmet dinners in the finest restaurants, who sent gifts that would make an Arab sheik blush, who said they would be with you through thick and thin, have now put you on "C.O.D." and are considering cutting off shipments of the raw materials essential to the completion of your finished products. These materials could be sold and ultimately converted into

1

cash, thereby reducing your problem. The vendors, however, are concerned because they found out you were "thin."

You are certain that you have the plague and that everyone out there is bent on destroying both you and your company.

Finally, there are the "vultures" who have heard about your problem and seek to remove the few precious dollars remaining in your vaults. These are the most dangerous because, contrary to popular belief, they do not have beady black eyes and a black mustache to match, and many of them do not even come from Chicago or New York. Insidiously, they may take the form of a middle man who for a "small fee" can provide you with instant access to all sorts of money. They may be unscrupulous attorneys who will generate considerable fees by enticing you down the path toward bankruptcy when this is not the appropriate course of action. They may be consultants who promise to cut your costs by 90 percent even though they are not familiar with your current staffing levels or the nature of your business.

If this scenario sounds familiar, as it does at some point in the lifetime of almost every company, you need to learn how to survive.

This book is dedicated both to the ulcer-ridden and heart attack–prone executives who are experiencing a business crisis right now, and to those executives with healthy companies who want to be better prepared for hard times when they come. For they *will* come and, in my experience, usually after some very profitable years that often take the edge off the key executives' leadership.

The crucial elements that determine the long-term survival of a company are the ways in which the company plans for and handles its crisis.

It is my contention, born of years of painful "hands-on" experience, that "Crisis Management" (CM) is in fact a science. Unfortunately, it is not sufficiently emphasized in the curriculum of the traditional graduate business school.

When a company is confronted with serious financial problems, it becomes necessary to abandon the more traditional approaches to management. Profit and loss control become less important, and budgets often lose their significance. The balance sheet, that strange document you always wanted to know about but were afraid to ask, suddenly looms in importance.

You learn about "street fighting" and what it really means; you learn the true meaning of strategy and "downside risk"; you learn to make the crisis your ally. But most of all, *you learn to survive*—sometimes when there is no other justification for that survival but the skills you will learn in this book.

So fasten your seatbelts and experience a new business adventure that will help to make you a better executive.

Chapter 2

Buying Time

Your creditors are stretched out as far as possible, threatening not to supply you with products. Your major lender intends to call in your loan. Cash is rapidly drying up, and you hear rumblings that some of your key people are getting discouraged. It is hard to produce in an efficient manner because product shortages often shut down your lines. The monthly and weekly reports you need to run your business are too late for meaningful actions, and it seems that the information they provide is not relevant to the problems that must be solved on a daily and sometimes hourly basis. The board of directors, growing nervous, is putting substantial pressure on you. Some board members have indicated they may resign. Your world is crumbling. Your attorneys shake their heads and suggest you talk to a bankruptcy attorney, who in turn may suggest that a chapter proceeding is your only solution. Your so-called business friends show up less often. You have a strange feeling of being isolated and deserted.

It is at this point that you must distance yourself to assess where you really are.

Unfortunately, when you're feeling surrounded on all sides, it is hard to think of a way to buy time. The resolution of this problem isn't easy. For many of you, it will mean a change in personality. The hard facts of life are that *you and only you* are the one most sincerely interested in both your own survival and that of the company. Everyone else, in a sense, has a conditional interest.

The bankers want to get their loan repaid. They can take collateral and force you to sell off valuable assets, thereby generating cash to further reduce the loan balance. Rather than admit within their own organization that a mistake was made either in granting you additional credit or in failing to stay on top of your operations, they find it easier to cast the blame on the "competence" and "credibility" of your management. These are code words the bank may use to convince you to be their "goat" and bow out.

The shareholders, on the other hand, care quite a bit about the future viability of the company. They know that the bank's tightening up and selling of valuable assets may transfer corporate wealth from their hands into those of the banks or financial institutions involved. However, like the bank, they might be happy to have your head if they had the power to obtain it.

The vendors are in direct competition with the banks for the same scarcely available cash. Pay the vendors and you will receive essential raw materials; pay the bank and you may be out of business. Upset the bank enough, and they may take steps that could also put you out of business.

In examining the question of conditional interest, you must distinguish between "vultures" and useful advisers. Advisers are dealing with many potential conflicts. Some of these conflicts, unfortunately, will not be in your best interest. Let me name just a few so that you can be on the alert:

1. They are concerned about maintaining their reputation in their professional community.
2. They are concerned about your paying them and may feel a need to stay on your good side.

3. The service that maximizes their fee may not necessarily be the service that provides you with optimum benefits.
4. They often rely on financial institutions as a source of business. Possibly they rely on the bank you are currently using.
5. Their clients may include some of your vendors and/or major stockholders.

Therefore, if at all possible, avoid engaging new advisers who have been recommended by banks and financial institutions, stockholders, or vendors, unless they have been carefully scrutinized. Conscientious, knowledgeable advisers are essential, but make certain that their allegiance is to your company and its long- and short-term survival.

In an atmosphere of conflict, how does an executive buy time? How is the bank enlisted as a working partner rather than as an adversary? How is the vendor given enough confidence in the company to deliver supplies? How is the fear of the stockholders allayed? How does the executive keep his or her own sanity in the face of adversity?

Fortunately, there are certain guidelines that can be followed. Before explaining in detail what they are and why they are necessary, let me list them here:

1. Find out as quickly as possible what your bankers, shareholders, vendors, and advisers stand to lose if the *worst* should happen. In other words, evaluate and quantify the nightmare. Allow your mind to head directly into the hurricane.
2. List every one of your fears. Leave no stone unturned until you know the best way to deal with each of them. Do not waste time seeking justice, fairness, and the good will of others. The destiny of your company is in *your* hands.
3. Make the crisis your ally. Be assertive and take the lead. Inform all those who need to know that there *is* a problem but that you can and will solve it. Let them know how implacable you can be if they will not cooperate. Telling

the world that all is fine when everyone knows that Rome is crumbling weakens your credibility. Subconsciously, everyone wants you to take the lead and reassure them.

4. Quickly develop, in written form, a program to present to all interested parties. At a minimum, it should include:

   a. Programs for reducing expenses
   b. Programs for increasing the flow of funds
   c. Changes in management and organization
   d. Pro forma profit and loss, cash-flow, and balance sheet statements
   e. Supporting assumptions
   f. A plan of short-term corporate strategy and, if appropriate, a somewhat longer-term outlook
   g. A careful explanation of reasons for past problems, internal as well as external
   h. A scheduling chart showing when all the above will be accomplished, and including assignments of executive responsibility

5. Analyze the results of guideline 1 above. Careful scrutiny of your findings will enable you to understand quickly the fears of the organizations and people who must deal with you. Remember, fear is a two-way street. Often the severely troubled company, when properly administered, can get better support than a healthier company. It's somewhat like saying to a bully, "If you hit me real hard, I'll throw up all over you."

It is important to keep in mind that the completion of guidelines 4a to 4g is less urgent than the completion of 4h. The banks and other interested parties must know that restoration and revitalization are in motion. There is simply not enough time to get all the work done first.

Handled properly, the implementation of these five guidelines normally will buy time. Of course, you must act promptly in the implementation of guideline 4. Let us now discuss each of these guidelines in greater detail.

ASSESSING YOUR LOSSES

In order to determine the losses that your banks or financial institutions and vendors will realize, it is necessary to make a careful evaluation of the balance sheet on the assumption that the liquidation of your company will take place. Tables 2-1 and 2-2, to be discussed in greater detail shortly, show a simple way to arrive at the assessment of losses. Keep in mind that at this point, this assessment is not meant to be a formal analysis for presentation to anyone. It is merely intended to give you an assessment of what your bankers, creditors, and shareholders stand to lose if you do not survive. While this may sound like backwards logic, the worse off they are, the better your leverage.

The quickest way to do this analysis is first to list the assets and liabilities from your latest balance sheet. From this, make a mental assumption that your company will be liquidating its assets promptly.

There are two basic classes of creditors who must be considered. First there are the priority creditors, who, by law, have first claim on your assets. Because of the complexity involved in dealing with priority problems, you may need qualified legal counsel to guide you. Normally included in the classification of priority creditors are payroll and related taxes as well as taxes owed to various state and federal government agencies. Second in line are the secured creditors, who are entitled to claim those assets they hold as security against your loan. (By the way, it is a good idea to have your attorneys check the supporting documentation to ascertain that the creditors have in fact taken the proper steps in obtaining their security.)

Column 1 in Table 2-1 shows the balance on the books of the company in accordance with generally accepted accounting principles on a going-concern basis. The problem with this method of accounting is that we are no longer dealing with a going concern. Let us take a moment to discuss each of the asset and liability accounts.

Cash on the books is the most liquid and usable of the assets of a going concern. Creditors wish to convert other assets to cash as soon as possible. In many cases a troubled company has been carefully managing float so that while there is a small positive balance on the books of the bank, the company is, in fact, in an overdraft position. This overdraft is in effect a zero-interest loan provided by the bank. It is possible the bank could become an unsecured creditor with respect to this overdraft if the problem is not promptly solved.

Accounts receivable is the next major asset. In a normal operating situation, creditors pay bills in a generally orderly manner, and an appropriate reserve is established specifically for older accounts or is based on some historical percentage. Unfortunately, once the news gets out that a company is in financial trouble, creditors begin to make unreasonable claims, products are returned for various and sundry reasons, and payments are significantly delayed. It is for this reason that the troubled company is unable to realize the full value of this asset.

The third major current asset classification is inventory. Invariably this asset deteriorates more than any other current asset. The deterioration is greatest if a significant portion of the inventory is in the work-in-process state. If raw materials are composed of commonly used items, they may retain a good portion of their value. One would think that finished items bring the most value; but what if the company's product is obsolete or has been legislated out of existence? Owners of companies are shocked when they are offered 25 to 30 percent for their investment from responsible purchasers.

Fixed assets present a more complex problem because certain fixed assets have actually *appreciated*. Since generally accepted accounting principles require those assets to be carried at cost less depreciation, they are often a source of additional funds. This is often the case when a company owns land. Sometimes, in our inflationary economy, some special equipment has either increased in value or not depreciated at the rate established in the accounting systems. Other fixed assets,

TABLE 2-1
The Harried Company
Analysis of Losses
($000)

	(1) Book Balance	(2) Elimination for Secured and Priority Creditors	(3) Elimination for Value Loss	(4) Balance for Unsecured Credit
Assets				
Cash	$ 775	$ 600[1]		$ 18
Accounts receivable—net	3,209	157[2]		3,209
Inventories	17,292		$8,646[3]	8,646
Other	964			965
Total current assets	22,240			
Property, plant, and equipment	16,224	14,000[4]	1,779[5]	445
Allowance for depreciation	4,890	4,200[4]	552[5]	138
Net fixed assets	11,334	9,800[4]	1,227[5]	307
Investments and other	6,445		3,867[6]	2,578
	$40,019			$15,722

Liabilities and Equity			
Accounts payable	$ 5,696		$ 5,696
Accrued liabilities	1,138	600[1]	538
Notes payable—unsecured[7]	3,600		3,600
Notes payable—secured	8,843	1,960[8]	6,883
Current portion of long-term debt	4,598		4,598
Accrued taxes	157	157[2]	—
Total current liabilities	24,032		21,315
Long-term debt	16,367		16,367
Net worth	(380)		
Total liabilities and equity	$40,019		$37,682

[1]The accrued liabilities include $600,000 payroll, which is a priority item. It is assumed that cash is used to pay off this debt.

[2]Federal taxes due are also priority items to be paid out of current assets.

[3]Inventories will be worth 50¢ per $1.00 upon liquidation.

[4]The note is secured by fixed assets having a net book value of $9,800,000.

[5]The remaining unsecured fixed assets are worth 20¢ per $1.00 upon liquidation.

[6]Investments and other are worth 40¢ per $1.00 upon liquidation.

[7]Shareholders are in last position after priority creditors, secured creditors, and unsecured creditors.

[8]The bank's secured notes payable are supported by assets worth 20¢ per $1.00 upon liquidation.

such as leasehold improvements, are often quite worthless when a company is considering a liquidation. In general, if land is not a major component of the total net value of fixed assets, there is a deterioration in value in relation to amounts carried on the books.

Investment accounts are also carried at cost, and the amounts in this classification can vary considerably. Once a company finds itself in financial difficulty, it is common to convert assets in investments into more liquid assets so that they can be utilized in the day-to-day operation of the business. The balance is, therefore, typically small by the time a liquidation analysis is made.

Payables are one of the most significant liability accounts. The company in trouble has typically extended the accounts payable to vendors as far as it will go. When an involuntary bankruptcy finally occurs, the extension is probably beyond the breaking point. It is the vendors in this account who stand to lose the most if the company fails. Their debt is typically unsecured, and, as I will discuss later, they are often the last to know. The balance in this account not only retains its value but often increases as vendors add interest and other charges and file lawsuits, and as contingent liabilities get converted to actual liabilities. Somehow, all liabilities "creep out of the woodwork" when a company is in trouble. The reasoning used above also applies to the accrued liabilities account. Our next major liability category is the note holders: long-term and short-term, secured and unsecured.

The secured note holders will normally begin to take steps to protect their collateral. Typically, bank loans are secured, in some manner, by accounts receivable, inventory, and, in some cases, fixed assets. The values are generally quite accurate and are reflected in the troubled company's accounting records. Even if a company initially had an unsecured revolving line of credit, by the time liquidation is under consideration, the banks have taken the steps to protect their loan. In fact, in most private companies the financial institutions have probably obtained personal guarantees from the troubled owners.

Notes in an unsecured state suffer the same fate as those of unsecured vendors. Any unsecured lines of credit and notes held by a financial institution are often the result of inattention on the part of the institution. If the borrower's trouble was identified early, the financial institution would normally take the necessary steps to secure the debt. Therefore, in many cases, the only remaining unsecured notes payable at the time liquidation is considered are the vendors', who have converted their accounts payable into longer-term notes. Accrued taxes are another account that is generally accurate. Accountants in a troubled company are very careful to review all taxes that are due the various government and regulatory agencies.

In general, the net impact is a serious reduction of the real net worth.

Column 2 in Table 2-1 recognizes the priority and secured creditors. For simplicity, let us assume that the bank is the holder of the notes payable and that the secured portion of the bank's debt is represented by fixed assets having a net book value of $9,800,000. Accrued payroll of $600,000 and taxes of $157,000 are further assumed to be paid off by utilizing current assets.

Reference note 4 shows a reduction in the net fixed assets by $9,800,000 to secure the notes payable. Eliminating these net assets requires an entry of $14,000,000 for property, plants, and equipment, less a depreciation allowance of $4,200,000. The remaining balance of $1,534,000 is, therefore, all that is available for the unsecured creditors at this stage. The balance is further reduced in column 3. Of the accrued liabilities, $600,000 is represented by payroll, which has priority over all other creditors. It is assumed that the company will use its most liquid asset, cash, to pay off this liability. This reduces the available cash to $175,000 and reduces the accrued liability account to $538,000. The entry in column 3 for federal taxes of $157,000 is also a priority item and virtually consumes the remaining cash available in the business. Unsecured creditors have lost the availability of over $10,500,000 in assets at the conclusion of the column 2 analysis.

Column 3 in Table 2-1 deals with the harsh realities of the real world. Once you liquidate, the value of your assets declines and even your secured creditor is less secured than he or she thought. For example, while the bank had $8,843,000 in debt secured by $9,800,000 in net fixed assets, those assets are only worth $1,960,000 upon liquidation. The rest of the bank's debt, namely $6,883,000, now becomes part of the total unsecured debt the company owes. Inventories which would be worth more if converted into finished goods and sold in an orderly manner are currently in different states: raw material, work in process, and finished goods. The effective value of this inventory is, under these conditions, generally dramatically reduced; we have assumed a reduction to 50 percent of the cost in this example. We further assume that investments and other assets decline to 40 percent of cost if a liquidation is necessary.

A few comments about the reference notes in column 3 should be made. Double-entry bookkeeping is no longer applicable. The inventory entry simply results in an $8,646,000 deterioration. There is no offsetting benefit or liability. Thus there are less assets for everyone, the bank's unsecured position increases, and so the total unsecured debt also increases. In a similar manner, other investments are reduced by $3,867,000 to a new reduced value of $2,578,000.

Using the results of the preliminary analysis in Table 2-1, let us see how everyone makes out if they force you to "throw in the towel." The analysis in Table 2-2 shows that the bank's total secured debt of $8,843,000 is only worth $1,960,000. This fact creates an unsecured liability of $6,883,000, which will ultimately be merged with the other unsecured creditors. The bank can, therefore, expect to collect $1,960,000 plus an additional 39.1¢ per $1.00 recovery, or $2,691,000, because of its participation as an unsecured creditor, as we shall see. The

TABLE 2-2
The Harried Company
Estimated Losses by Class
($000)

		Loss
1. *The Secured Creditor*		
Total secured debt	$ 8,843	
Market value of security	1,960	
Unsecured portion	6,883	
Recovery		
Sale of security	$ 1,960	
Participation with other unsecured creditors		
(6,883 × 39.1%)	2,691	
Total Recovery	$ 4,651	$ 4,192
(4,651/8,843 = 52.6¢ per $1.00)		
2. *The Unsecured Creditor*		
Total unsecured debt	$37,682	
Realizable from asset liquidation	15,722	
Related fees of liquidation	1,100	
Net Proceeds for Unsecured Creditors	$14,722	$22,960
(14,722/37,682 = 39.1¢ per $1.00)		
3. *The Shareholder*		
Loss is total. No recovery.		

total recovery of the bank's debt is $4,651,000, or 52.6¢ per dollar. If the company liquidates, the bank could lose in excess of $4,000,000. After all the revisions were made in columns 2 and 3 of Table 2-1, the unsecured creditors had $15,722,000 available to distribute to creditors who are owed $37,682,000. We have assumed various liquidation expenses—commissions, professional fees, court costs, etc.—totalling $1,000,000. The net market value of $14,722,000 provides a settlement of 39.1¢ per dollar to the unsecured creditors.

At last you have quantified the nightmare. The secured creditors are going to lose $4,192,000, and the unsecured cred-

itors will lose $22,960,000. The secured and unsecured credi-
tors, of course, will have to be segregated by specific company
and financial institution. Believe it or not, many of your creditors do not understand the financial risks they are taking by
not cooperating with you. On a selective basis, it may become
necessary to let them know the facts as you see them. The
shareholders, alas, are left holding the bag with very little left
but anger.

LIST YOUR FEARS

This list is a very private one. You are a unique individual.
You have, written or unwritten, a philosophy of life. Fears of
potential legal action against you may flash through your mind.
You may be concerned about your health. Will the effort and
stress you now feel and may feel in the future take a physio-
logical toll? What will your family, friends, and business asso-
ciates think of you? Do you fear economic ruin, or a dramatic
change in your standard of living? Does the company represent your sense of "self"? Can you make a mental distinction
between your life and well-being and that of the company?

These questions may seem out of place in a book on business and management. But just as you have quantified your
losses by following guideline 1, so too must you face and deal
with your fears, both real or imagined.

My general suggestions are:

1. Seek *no* advice in making your initial list. The fact that an
   adviser or confidant of yours tells you that he or she is comfortable about a certain matter doesn't necessarily mean
   that *you* are comfortable with it. The "hot seat" is yours.
   No one else really knows what it feels like.
2. Assume the worst in each situation. Seek *competent* advice
   until you feel certain that you are dealing with the matter
   in the best possible way. If you have legal fears, learn what
   real actions you might face, how you could deal with them,
   and what would be the most likely outcome.

3. Consider various relaxation techniques and exercises such as jogging to help reduce the level of stress you must face.
4. Talk honestly with your family and friends. Share your problems and feelings. This may bring you closer to them.
5. Carefully evaluate your economic situation:
  a. What is your net worth?
  b. What form does it take?
  c. How well protected is it?
  d. What is your general market value?
  e. How would you handle yourself financially if things got worse?

Having given full vent to the pessimist that is in all of us, take the papers and notes, put them aside, and breathe a sigh of relief. You have mentally made the trip through the storm, discovered that you will survive, and can now turn to greener pastures. Your head is out of the sand. You are ready to see the crisis in a new light—how it will become your ally rather than your enemy.

MAKE THE CRISIS YOUR ALLY

Fortified by the results of following guidelines 1 and 2, you are ready to deal with your would-be adversaries and make them your partners in an important venture where everyone can benefit. At this point in time, it is essential that you believe in the basic viability of your business—that you believe that with the proper support of vendors, bankers, and shareholders, there is a business worth saving. In Chapter 3, the question of viability will be studied with greater intensity. Now, however, the fundamental belief in the future of your business must be communicated to all concerned. You will not be very convincing unless (1) you believe intensely in your company *and* (2) you are willing to make the effort required to see the project through. Remember that at this juncture you have probably not worked out a presentable corporate strategy or meaningful financial forecats. Most likely, you are just beginning to wrestle with the task of cost cutting, realizing with great pain that some of your loyal and trusted employees may have to be fired.

It is time to contact the bank and some of the key vendors and set up *separate* meetings to update them on the status of the company. Let them know that things have been tight. Reassure them that you have a program to deal with the problem and that you will require their support and cooperation. Do not apologize. Do not beg. Politely, but firmly, make it clear you "expect" and "know" you will get their support. Set up these meetings as far into the future as you can. Your knowledge of their economic risks (derived from guideline 1) may prove useful. One word of caution: Never use threats and never "personalize" your requests. Fundamentally, you are dealing with business recommendations, which, given the unpleasant circumstances, represent the best alternative course of action for all concerned.

DEVELOP THE GENERAL PROGRAM

At separate meetings with the bank and certain key creditors, it will be necessary to present a brief overall program with timetables and schedules. This will show them that you are in control. Do at least the following, and type and distribute the information:

1. Explain the fundamental internal and external conditions that created the crisis in the first place. These could include changes in the general economy, competition, government regulations, loss of key people, and lack of good financial control. Explain, in general terms, what you are doing to deal with each of these conditions *now*.

2. Quickly list all areas where action has already been taken, clearly defining the action, the anticipated benefits, and when those benefits will be reflected in the financial statements.

3. Describe those activities and operations planned for cur-

tailment or reduced levels of operation. Indicate when decisions will be made in that area.

4. Summarize any significant changes in organization structure, responsibility, authority, and/or reporting relationships.

5. Seriously consider having the top people take a temporary reduction in compensation during the crisis to help communicate, both internally and externally, the sincerity of the austerity program.

6. Discuss the sale of certain non-income-producing assets, if appropriate, for the generation of cash. Indicate the possible dollar value and estimated time involved to complete the various sales transactions.

7. Describe the types of financial controls that will be used to supplement your current system throughout the crisis.

8. Discuss, in general, programs for the quick sale of certain inventories to generate cash, for a reduction of the collection cycle, and for the short-term stretching of accounts payable.

9. Specify a date when a corporate strategy and pro forma financial statements with supporting assumptions will be completed.

10. Describe each of the above as projects that are in motion. Using a PERT- or CPM-type chart, show how these projects tie together, who will be responsible for each project, and when the projects will be completed.

11. Let your bank or financial institution know what you want from them. For example, you may want them to:
    a. Maintain current level of financing for the next X months until the projects are completed.
    b. Provide certain guarantees.
    c. Extend additional credit for obtaining additional collateral or guarantees.
    d. Defer interest payments for X months.
    e. Accept transfer of certain assets directly to the financial institution in return for debt reduction.
    f. Convert a portion of the debt from short to long term.

12. Let key creditors also know what you want from them. You may want:

a. Continuation of existing terms or extended terms for the next X months until the projects are completed.

b. Possible conversion of some existing debt, if it is substantial, into some form of a note.

c. Possible marketing arrangements to provide mutual benefits to both you and your creditor. For example, company A, the company in crisis, owed company B a substantial amount of money. Company B supplied the major raw material ingredients for company A's final product. Company B encouraged its own dealer network to buy company A's finished product. A percentage of the proceeds from these sales was used to "pay down" the old debt in addition to paying for current merchandise. In six months, company A had paid off its old debt and was current on its new debt. At the same time, company B both increased its sales volume and cured a possible problem account. This cooperative venture took imagination on the part of both companies. Their combined efforts went a long way in helping company A back on its feet.

FEAR—THE TWO-WAY STREET

If all goes well at these preliminary meetings, you will be granted the time needed to concentrate on the areas discussed in subsequent chapters. In my experience, if you are honest, stay on top of the problem, and offer hope for a solution in a reasonable period of time, you will get cooperation.

If that cooperation is not forthcoming, you must be prepared to take a tough stance. Remember, your economic survival may be at stake. When someone is about to drive a sword into your heart, you do not ask him about his philosophy of life until he has been disarmed and subdued.

If you have carefully assessed your situation by following

guidelines 1 and 2, it may be necessary to initiate the process of "street fighting." Please understand, dear reader, that I do not recommend this unless there is no other way. Be prepared to follow through on any statements you make. Save the grandstanding and emotional outbursts for the theater; this is "for real." Here are some ideas that have proven successful:

1. Personally threaten to resign, possibly with some other key people, and let the bank or vendor run the company.
2. Inform those on the other side of the table that you are considering filing for bankruptcy. Also let them know their expected losses, should this occur.
3. If there are legal considerations working in your favor, let them be known, after proper advice from counsel.

Psychologically, it is important for your would-be adversary to make a clear distinction between you as an "individual" and you as "your company." This clarification will get their attention and enable you to take their criticisms less personally.

AN EXAMPLE

In Exhibit 2-1 I have shown a specific example of a short-term operating plan. The report should be reviewed section by section to get the basic concept clearly formed.

Section I, *Overview*, summarizes, in this case, what the company's alternatives are and what the proposed action plan includes. It briefly describes what the company has to offer and the problems that a new investor must face. Also, Section I summarizes the probable benefits that would occur by accepting this plan. Section II, *Program Responsibility and Timing*, shows in the format of critical path scheduling the projects to be performed, the timing, and the individuals responsible for supervision. It also indicates that projects are already underway and shows their relative stage of completion. Section III, *Sell Idle Properties*, is supported by a chart showing the following for each idle property: location, net cost basis, encumbrances, net value obligations, and probable timing for disposal. Section IV, *Sell Certain Assets and Transfer Certain Liabilities,* is similar to Section III and includes the transfer of certain assets and liabilities to the financial institution. Section V, *Revise Acquisition Package,* emphasizes that a package (similar to that discussed in Chapter 4) must be developed once the proposed program is approved. Section VI, *Make Composition with Creditors,* explains how the company intends to get creditors to accept less than 100¢ on the dollar. Section VII, *Make Operating Plan for Corporate and Local Plant and Other Projects,* summarizes the cost implications of the plan by time period. In a troubled company, the interval is usually by week. Section VII describes the major feature of the plan. Section VIII, *New Loan Agreement,* finally states what the company requires from its financial institution to finance the plan and the related workout. Sometimes, when rates of manufacturing have to be reduced, it is important to show that the company has a careful understanding of its break-even levels. An example of a break-even analysis is in the Appendix of Exhibit 2-1.

EXHIBIT 2-1

I — OVERVIEW

Over the past many months PQ management has embarked on a program of phasing out all unprofitable entities while seeking a corporate or individual investor based on the guidelines set forth in the bank's letter.

PQ management has seriously evaluated the three major alternatives open to the company:

1. A formal filing
2. An acquisition or equity investment
3. A plan of retrenchment which places the company in the best position to implement alternative 2

The proposal in this report deals with our recommendation to proceed with alternative 3. It is an action plan which involves:

1. Debt cancellation of approximately X million of assets from the sale of idle facilities and certain net assets
2. Implementation of a cost-reduction plan which has been over 50 percent completed, involving termination of production and corporate personnel and transfer of PQ production to the PQ-1 wholly owned subsidiary
3. Completion of the composition with creditors utilizing certain collateral
4. Revision of the acquisition package for new investors

The remaining debt balance of approximately X_2 million would then be converted to a new loan agreement.

A number of firms have expressed serious interest in the company, and we have learned from this experience the requirements for making the company more attractive to new investors. The assets of PQ which have the greatest appeal are:

1. The PQ brand-name acceptance with the consumer, rated by many as second in the industry.
2. The PQ-2 operation outside the United States.
3. The PQ-1 operation in the Northwest.
4. The opportunity to utilize the net operating loss carry-forward.
5. The local plant serving an independent dealer network. Its ability to generate profits appears to be an accepted assumption by most investors. (It has a break-even level of 4 units per day.)

(continued)

EXHIBIT 2-1 (*continued*)

The new investor, however, faces certain obstacles. They are:

1. Diversion from the management's primary objective of making the operating entities profitable in order to deal with the disposal of idle facilities and the disposition of certain distributor outlets
2. Evaluation of exposure related to creditors, settlements, and other contingent liabilities

The basic plan we are proposing fundamentally overcomes these obstacles and provides the new investor with a viable entity. The new entity can operate through the slow part of the season, according to the plan, and be profitable for the fiscal year.

These profits are derived from PQ-2 and PQ-1 which have generated a profit of X_3 million for four months ending _____. These corporations will benefit from the injection of PQ product, which should increase the total profit dollars generated as well as improve the profit margins through the recovery of fixed expenses.

The plan anticipates that at the end of December a decision would be made to either sell, start up, or maintain the local plant. This decision would be based on the corporate outlook, economic outlook, order backlog conditions at that time, and the importance of maintaining the net operating loss carry-forward. We believe approval of this plan would:

1. Maximize the probability of an acquisition
2. Maximize realization on sale of idle assets
3. Create a surviving entity that can generate sufficient cash flow and profits
4. Provide the basis for an equity conversion that could have significant future value

II — PROGRAM RESPONSIBILITY AND TIMING

Shown in Figure 2-1 is an activity flowchart which identifies the primary tasks and milestones. It illustrates, moreover, how these activities interrelate with each other. Each major grouping has been assigned a project number and put under the direct responsibility of one individual. They are:

Project	Description	Responsibility
1	Sell idle assets to bank	A
2	Sell certain outlet assets to bank	B

EXHIBIT 2-1 (*continued*)

3	Revise acquisition package	C
4	Make composition with creditors	D
5	Make operating plan for PQ	C
	a. Production cutback	C
	b. Corporate cutback	C
	c. Transfer of activities to PQ-1	B
6	Other	
	a. Meet financing and operational needs of PQ-2 and PQ-1	C
	b. Renegotiate insurance	D

Project 5 is currently about 50 percent complete; the plans have been developed for all other projects awaiting authorization from the bank to proceed.

We believe the accounting and legal work for the first two projects can be completed within a few weeks. This is also true for developing a revised acquisition package. Project 4 will probably require 60 to 90 days for completion. The operating plan for PQ is already in motion with major reductions underway. The only areas that cannot be immediately reduced are accounting and the use of production personnel to finish up the last X_4 units in process which the bank has approved.

It is important that our subsidiaries receive assistance particularly in the financing area and that insurance premiums be renegotiated as shown in Project 6. These activities should take place within the next 60 days.

III — SELL IDLE PROPERTIES (PROJECT 1)

Shown in Schedule 2-1 are the proposed idle properties to be transferred to the bank. The selling price is X_5 million, which is equal to the cost basis of the properties shown. The proceeds would be applied to the cancellation of existing debt. The schedule shows the cost basis less related encumbrances. It also shows the monthly payments and summarizes the primary terms of each lease and mortgage. PQ personnel would, upon request, assist the bank in the disposal of these assets. A summary of the real estate firms who have the related listings will be provided to the bank.

(continued)

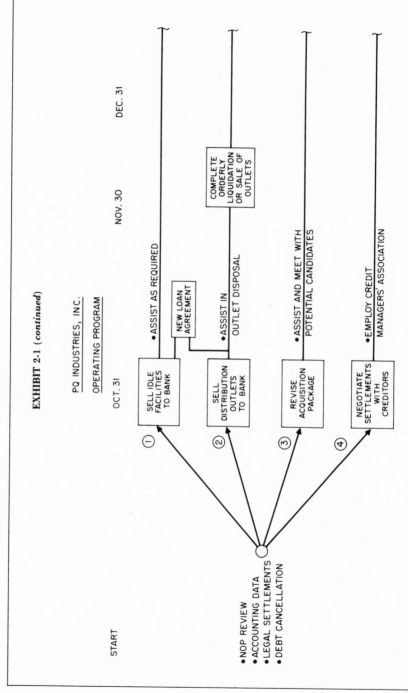

EXHIBIT 2-1 (*continued*)

PQ INDUSTRIES, INC.

OPERATING PROGRAM

START   OCT. 31   NOV. 30   DEC. 31

• NOP REVIEW
• ACCOUNTING DATA
• LEGAL SETTLEMENTS
• DEBT CANCELLATION

① SELL IDLE FACILITIES TO BANK
    • ASSIST AS REQUIRED
    NEW LOAN AGREEMENT

② SELL DISTRIBUTION OUTLETS TO BANK
    • ASSIST IN OUTLET DISPOSAL
    COMPLETE ORDERLY LIQUIDATION OR SALE OF OUTLETS

③ REVISE ACQUISITION PACKAGE
    • ASSIST AND MEET WITH POTENTIAL CANDIDATES

④ NEGOTIATE SETTLEMENTS WITH CREDITORS
    • EMPLOY CREDIT MANAGERS' ASSOCIATION

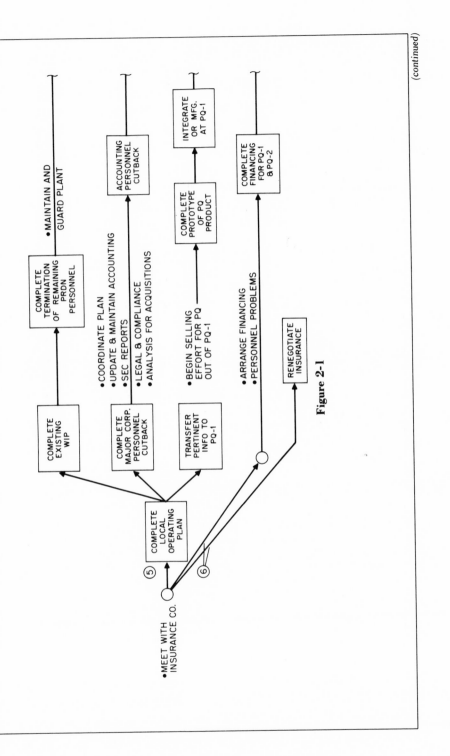

Figure 2-1

(continued)

EXHIBIT 2-1 (*continued*)

SCHEDULE 2-1
PQ Industries, Inc.
Sale of Nonoperating Properties

Net Cost Basis	Encum- brances	Cost Value Net of Encum- brances	Payments (M: Monthly; S: Semiannually; A: Annually)	Duration	Terms of Lease or Mortgage

Totals

EXHIBIT 2-1 (*continued*)

IV — SELL CERTAIN ASSETS AND TRANSFER CERTAIN LIABILITIES (PROJECT 2)

While PQ is currently operating outlets in locations A, B, C, D, and E, there exist assets in the nonoperating outlets as well. The plan, which is shown in Schedule 2-2, is to sell to the bank the net accounts receivable, inventories, property, plant and equipment, and certain other noncurrent assets primarily composed of reserves and rental-site deposits. The bank would also reduce the amount paid for the assets by any unsecured liabilities it would be assuming. The total debt cancellation would be $\$X_6$ million represented by special financing, long-term debt, and the net purchase of assets.

In order to complete the composition of creditors, we request that the first $\$X_7$ million from the sale of these assets be set aside in a special fund to be used, with bank approval, for that purpose and to cover certain established operating expenses. Any surplus funds would be returned to the bank. The setting aside of these dollars is reflected in the selling price and shown in Schedule 2-2.

Decisions would have to be made to either sell or liquidate in an orderly manner each outlet, and we would be prepared to assist the bank with operating data and personnel in this endeavor at their request. We estimate savings to the bank of between $\$X_8$ and $\$X_9$ million under an orderly program in comparison to alternative 1 discussed in Section I.

V — REVISE ACQUISITION PACKAGE (PROJECT 3)

Upon approval of this plan in its existing or modified form, a new package should be developed for corporate and individual investors. It will emphasize more comprehensively the ability of the local plant to generate profits, the PQ market position and consumer rating, the use of the net operating loss carry-forward, and the future potential of PQ-1 and PQ-2. The package will avoid the need to review and evaluate idle facilities and stores. This will shorten the review period acquired by an investor.

Certain investors that the company previously spoke to have indicated a renewed interest based on an oral discussion of this proposed plan. Because the plan enables PQ to operate under different conditions, it allows the acquisition to be pursued in an orderly environment that can provide the best price for the revised corporation.

This project can be completed within a few weeks.

(continued)

EXHIBIT 2-1 (*continued*)

SCHEDULE 2-2
PQ Industries, Inc.
Sale of Certain Assets and Transfer of Certain Liabilities

	Values at Locations										Real Estate	Total
	A	B	C	D	E	F	G	H	I	J		
Assets												
Net—Accounts Receivable	—	—	—	—	—	—	—	—	—	—	—	—
Inventories[1]												
New product	—	—	—	—	—	—	—	—	—	—	—	—
Trucks	—	—	—	—	—	—	—	—	—	—	—	—
Used and other	—	—	—	—	—	—	—	—	—	—	—	—
Parts and accessories	—	—	—	—	—	—	—	—	—	—	—	—
Rental (net)	—	—	—	—	—	—	—	—	—	—	—	—
Property, plant and equipment (net) and other	—	—	—	—	—	—	—	—	—	—	—	—
Other Noncurrent												
Reserves	—	—	—	—	—	—	—	—	—	—	—	—
Organization and deposits	—	—	—	—	—	—	—	—	—	—	—	—

Long-term receivables							
Rental site deposits and other							
Total Assets							
Less:							
Funds to be made available from the sale of collateral							
Total Assets Sold							
Additional liabilities to be cancelled:							
Accrued taxes and other							
Total Debt Cancellation							
Special financing[1]							
Long-term debt							
Other notes payable							
General obligation cancellation							

[1]These values are being continuously reduced.

(continued)

EXHIBIT 2-1 (*continued*)

VI — MAKE COMPOSITION WITH CREDITORS (PROJECT 4)

This project would probably take between 60 and 90 days to complete. It is, of course, difficult to estimate settlements before negotiations actually begin. Our objective initially would be to try to settle for amounts below the levels summarized in Schedule 2-3. Our approach in carrying out this task would be to:

1. Employ the Credit Managers' Association
2. Send out letters to the creditors establishing a meeting date (the meeting to be run by the CM Association)
3. Establish at the meeting a creditors' committee
4. Get approval of a plan from the creditors' committee
5. Negotiate with remaining dissenters

It is important to note that about one-half of the number of vendors in the corporate payables list are owed $500 or less, representing about $41,000. We have assumed a settlement with this group of 100¢ per dollar. The litigation settlements are very difficult to estimate; many cases are weak, and if settlements are not accelerated, the total dollar exposure should continue to reduce.

Our preliminary analysis indicates settlements could range between X_{10} and X_{11}. It is anticipated that funds would be provided from the sale of outlet inventory, as discussed in Section IV. We are also exploring the possibility of alternative settlements using long-term non-interest-bearing notes rather than cash.

It should be emphasized that the costs of implementing this project are more than offset by the benefits of Projects 1 and 2.

The company has developed the basic plan and contacted the Credit Managers' Association.

VII — MAKE OPERATING PLAN FOR CORPORATE AND LOCAL PLANT AND OTHER PROJECTS (PROJECTS 5 AND 6)

The basic operating plan has been completed and the disbursements only are shown in Schedule 2-4. The production department is finishing the units currently in the line which were approved by the bank and is already implementing the phase-out program which is part of the cash-flow summary shown in Schedule 2-4. We are beginning the staff reductions in corporate as outlined on that same schedule. It involves phasing out engineering; transferring the sales effort to PQ-1; and maintaining the accounting staff needed for SEC filings, financial reports, compliance, and special evaluations to record any asset sales and assist any

EXHIBIT 2-1 (*continued*)

SCHEDULE 2-3
PQ Industries, Inc.
Analysis of Liabilities

	Amount	Estimated Settlement	Approximate Number of Vendors
Corporate Payables			
Over $10,000	————	————	————
$5,000 to $9,999	————	————	————
$1,000 to $4,999	————	————	————
$500 to $999	————	————	————
Under $500	————	————	————
Distributive Outlet Payables			
Location A	————	————	————
Location B	————	————	————
Location C	————	————	————
Location D	————	————	————
Location E	————	————	————
Location F	————	————	————
Location G	————	————	————
Location H	————	————	————
Location I	————	————	————
Location J	————	————	————
Notes Payable and Other			
K	————	————	————
L	————	————	————
M	————	————	————

(*continued*)

EXHIBIT 2-1 (*continued*)

investor or acquirer in obtaining financial data during their review phase. Executive personnel are utilized as required to carry out the various projects spelled out in the operating plan.

A careful review of each expense category will show that the operating cost of following this plan is less than alternative 1. Accounting personnel and equivalent management cost would be required under any option, as well as most of the other expenses identified in Schedule 2-4. Certain areas will require special discussion, such as entering the industry shows.

Our plan involves idling the local plant through the slow part of the season and transferring the PQ production and sales effort to the PQ-1 plant.

A backlog of PQ demand would be developed through this period out of PQ-1, and once its ability to deliver is absorbed, the company would evaluate, with bank approval, the reopening of the local plant for the season. A decision should be made by the end of December to either start up the local plant, sell it, or keep it idle, depending on conditions at that time. In this decision it will be necessary to evaluate the net operating loss carry-forward.

PQ would coordinate the transfer of engineering plans and assist in the development of the prototypes for our product line. Sales of the PQ line would be conducted out of PQ-1. Production rates for filling the PQ backlog would be established. We have currently received approval of an X_{12} million contract which we will try to manufacture out of PQ-1. Our thought would be to establish a distribution arrangement between PQ-1 and PQ, wherein PQ receives a fixed percent of gross sales on PQ product.

In addition, there will be ongoing operational and financing problems for both PQ-1 and PQ-2. In the past, PQ management helped negotiate the revolving lines of credit for PQ-2 and established the retail financing contacts. PQ-1 and PQ-2, at this time, will continue to require assistance in this area. Personnel problems will probably continue to exist until there is some clear resolution in the minds of the employees related to the stability of the company.

If the basic structure of the plan is approved by the bank, we would again renegotiate our insurance and bonding costs and should obtain significant reductions.

VIII — NEW LOAN AGREEMENT

After the sale of the idle facilities and certain selected net assets of the distribution outlets to the bank, there will be a remaining loan balance. It is anticipated that this balance would be converted into a new

EXHIBIT 2-1 (*continued*)

SCHEDULE 2-4
PQ Industries
Projected Disbursements

								For Week Ending					
Category	10/19	10/26	11/2	11/9	11/16	11/23	11/30	12/7	12/14	12/21	12/28		
Payroll[1]	—	—	—	—	—	—	—	—	—	—	—		
Benefits	—	—	—	—	—	—	—	—	—	—	—		
Mortgage[2]	—	—	—	—	—	—	—	—	—	—	—		
Warranty	—	—	—	—	—	—	—	—	—	—	—		
Telephone	—	—	—	—	—	—	—	—	—	—	—		
Heat, light, and power	—	—	—	—	—	—	—	—	—	—	—		
Data processing	—	—	—	—	—	—	—	—	—	—	—		
Maintenance and supplies	—	—	—	—	—	—	—	—	—	—	—		
Travel and entertainment	—	—	—	—	—	—	—	—	—	—	—		
Taxes, licenses, rental, etc.	—	—	—	—	—	—	—	—	—	—	—		
Federal and state taxes	—	—	—	—	—	—	—	—	—	—	—		
Professional services[3]	—	—	—	—	—	—	—	—	—	—	—		
Director and shareholder costs	—	—	—	—	—	—	—	—	—	—	—		
General contingency	—	—	—	—	—	—	—	—	—	—	—		
Total	—	—	—	—	—	—	—	—	—	—	—		

[1]Direct labor and overhead labor scheduled to complete remaining work in process approved by bank not included.
[2]Costs related to maintaining collateral position in the local plant through December 31 (mortgages, _____; property taxes, _____) not included. Insurance expenses estimated at Y_1 through December 31; includes insurance for the outlets as well as the local plant. At this time the allocation of costs to the local plant and the renegotiated insurance cannot be fully determined because they depend upon the bank's action related to the plan.
[3]Does not include any fees and costs related to such uncontrollable items as mergers, defense against creditors, bankruptcy filing, or other unusual activity.

(continued)

35

EXHIBIT 2-1 (*continued*)

loan agreement which would enable the company to implement its operating plan and the composition of creditors. In Section IV, the company requested that the first X_7 million from the sale of inventory be set aside in a separate account to deal primarily with the composition of creditors and certain operating expenses. Any additional funds, if needed, can be obtained, with bank approval, from the distribution arrangements between PQ-1 and PQ. While many details would have to be worked out, the loan would provide for:

1. A waiver of interest on the new loan balance for one year
2. An agreement to provide necessary support for the PQ-1 and PQ-2 operations
3. The provision of proceeds from the sale of collateral for the composition of creditors

The remaining debt would be secured by the unsold assets and would primarily include PQ-1, PQ-2, and the local plant. The drafting of the structure of this agreement can begin immediately.

APPENDIX

Break-Even Evaluation of the Local Plant

Because it will be necessary to evaluate the reopening of the local plant as we approach the end of December, the analysis in Schedules 2-5 to 2-8 shows the plant's ability to generate profits. It shows a break-even level of 3.2 units per day, and its profit contribution at a volume of 12 per day. The plant has a normal capacity of about 24 units per day.

EXHIBIT 2-1

SCHEDULE 2-5
PQ Industries, Inc.
Local Pro Forma Income Statement
(at 12 units per day)

Sales		Total	Percentage
Units		264	
Dollars		1,111.9	100.0
Cost of Sales			
Material	483.6		
Labor	114.4		
Overhead	116.6	714.6	64.3
Gross Margin		397.3	35.7
Administrative and accounting	13.4		
Sales expenses	38.6		
Engineering expenses	12.7	64.7	5.8
Operating Profit		332.6	29.9

(continued)

EXHIBIT 2-1 (*continued*)

SCHEDULE 2-6
PQ Industries, Inc.
Local Plant

	Per Month
Administrative and Accounting	
Salaries and wages	$ 8,244
Payroll costs and fringe benefits	1,484
Travel and entertainment	200
Telephone	1,000
Dues and subscriptions	50
Data processing	1,000
Depreciation	800
Photocopying machines	400
Office supplies	200
	$13,378
Sales Expenses	
Salaries and wages	$13,720
Payroll costs and fringe benefits	2,470
Warranty expenses	7,000
Advertising	2,500
Cooperative media advertising	2,500
Brochures and catalogs	1,500
Shows and exhibits	2,000
Photocopying machines	800
Office supplies	200
Dues and subscriptions	100
Travel and entertainment	3,000
Telephone	2,000
Depreciation	800
	$38,590
Engineering Expenses	
Salaries and wages	$ 7,344
Payroll costs and fringe benefits	1,322
Supplies	1,000
Plan approvals	125
Travel and entertainment	500
Telephone	1,000
Heat, light, and power	250
Outside consultants	500
Rent: building	700
	$12,741

EXHIBIT 2-1 (*continued*)

SCHEDULE 2-7
PQ Industries, Inc.
Local Manufacturing
(Manufacturing Expenses Per Month)

Product Mix	Units
A	22
B	132
C	110
Total Monthly Production	264
Average Production Rate per Day	12

Manufacturing Expenses	Fixed	Variable	Total
Indirect labor (per schedule)	$24,150	$ 5,000	$ 29,150
Payroll taxes	3,000	11,355	14,355
Other fringes	500	11,500	12,000
Employee recruiting		200	200
Manufacturing supplies		5,280	5,280
Perishable tools		2,112	2,112
Stat., printing, and office supplies	250	250	500
Postage		300	300
Photocopying supplies		400	400
Maintenance and repairs— equipment,		2,700	2,700
buildings, and grounds	800		800
Trash pickup		675	675
Janitorial services and gardener	150	150	300
Travel and entertainment		200	200
Telephone	1,000	700	1,700
Heat, light, and power	1,500	1,500	3,000
Dues and subscription	50		50
Licenses and manufacturing permits	200		200
Rental: plant equipment		3,000	3,000
Vendor rework		700	700
Real estate and personal property taxes	7,300		7,300
Data processing expense	600	600	1,200
Insurance: general	8,000		8,000
Repair finished goods		2,500	2,500
Freight in		3,000	3,000
Gas and oil nontransport		200	200
Rent: building	1,600		1,600
Rent: land	500		500
Depreciation	14,650		14,650
Totals	$64,250	$52,322	$116,572

(continued)

EXHIBIT 2-1 (*continued*)

SCHEDULE 2-8
PQ Industries, Inc.
Break-Even Analysis of Local Plant

	Number of Units	Average per Unit	Total
Average Selling Price			
A	22	$9,699	$ 213,378
B	132	2,681	353,892
C	110	4,951	544,610
Total	264	$4,212	$1,111,880
Average Material Costs			
A	22	$3,914	$ 86,108
B	132	1,000	132,000
C	110	2,414	265,540
Total	264	$1,832	$483,648
Average Labor Costs			
A	22	$825	$18,150
B	132	192	25,344
C	110	442	48,620
Total	264	$349	$92,114

1. X = unit sales at break-even level
2. Local monthly overhead costs including administration, selling, and engineering = $128,959 + .57$ (direct labor dollars).
3. Variable cost per equivalent unit:

    Material $1,832
    Labor   349
                 ‾‾‾‾‾‾
                 $2,181

4. Direct labor dollars per month at break-even level = $349X$, so that overhead cost in step 2 can be redefined as $128,959 + .57 (349X)$.
5. Equivalent selling price per unit = $4,212.
6. Break-even level = $2,181 (X) + 128,959 + .57 (349X) = 4,212X$

    $$128,959 = 1,832X$$
    $$X = 70.4 \text{ units per month, or 3.2 units per day}$$

Having completed these steps properly, you have only accomplished one thing. You have bought time. In Chapter 3, we begin to use this time effectively for the benchmark meetings to be held in the near future with banks, financial institutions, creditors, and/or shareholders.

Using Time Effectively

Now that you have bought some time, you must review your current problems carefully in order to begin the task of maximizing internal cash flow. This chapter will guide you in these processes. Chapter 4 will help you select the appropriate form for a corporate strategy and financial plan.

Management must take a hard look at the situation promptly. It will be essential to gather accurate and current profit and loss, cash status, and balance sheet information, and to examine the cash-flow problem for the next six months. Seek out other internal sources of funds through such steps as:

- Sale of inventories
- Reduction of the collection cycle
- Sale of fixed assets
- Consolidation and shutdown of facilities
- Proper management of accounts payable
- Identification of areas for immediate revenue increase
- Identification of areas for cost reduction

The status of your existing relationship with your banker must be assessed. (When was the last time you personally met with your banker before your financial problems began?) Take a hard look at (1) your organizational structure, (2) job descriptions, including responsibilities and duties, and (3) the qualifi-

cations, reliability, and loyalty of your personnel. It will probably be necessary to consolidate jobs and let people go. You
may need to ask selected personnel to take compensation
reductions in order to retain their jobs.

Carefully evaluate the vendors who supply the material or
services you need to stay in business. How good is your rap-
port with them? Do you have alternative sources? Who are
the key vendors? Even a few unsecured creditors, if agitated,
could get together and put you into bankruptcy. It is essential
that you meet with qualified counsel to ensure your awareness
of any existing or potential legal problems. In certain cases
there are requirements for public disclosure that must be met
in a timely manner.

In effect, you are developing a short-term strategy for stay-
ing alive through this phase. These temporary measures do
not replace the full corporate strategy and financial plan that
will be discussed in Chapter 4, but you will never get that far
without using the intervening time effectively.

All this effort has one major purpose: to convince top- and
middle-management people inside the company, as well as the
outsiders who support you, that your business is viable and
worth saving. If management is not convinced of this, they will
behave like captains of a sinking ship: frantically busy, scur-
rying around, but fully convinced that they are going to
drown. This need to communicate with key employees at all
levels is often underestimated by the top executive. Your
chances of avoiding bankruptcy require tenacity at all levels.

To better illustrate how *the effective use of time* phase may
be carried out, let us study hypothetical company XYZ. Please
refer to Tables 3-1 and 3-2, which provide current profit and
loss and balance sheet information.

REVIEW EXISTING FINANCIAL STATEMENTS

Company XYZ imports products from the Far East and
purchases materials from all over the United States for ulti-

TABLE 3-1
Company XYZ
Profit and Loss
For Fiscal Year Ending _____
($000)

		Percentage
Sales	$5,712	100.0
Cost of sales	3,297	57.7
Gross profit	2,415	42.3
Selling expense	1,740	30.4
General and administrative expense	753	13.2
Total operating expenses	$2,493	43.7
Other income	12	
Loss before interest and taxes	$(66)	

mate domestic distribution in most of the continental 48 states. The most recent profit and loss statement (Table 3-1) shows sales of $5,712,000 and a net loss of $66,000 before interest and taxes. The rate of interest was (at that time) an exhorbitant 25 percent because of the company's financial condition.

The company believes it can maintain its current level of sales, but over the next 12 months it does not anticipate increased unit volume. New products would generate revenue, but they require a cash investment in excess of what company XYZ can afford and/or require a lead time that is too long.

The company, therefore, has to focus on improving the profit structure rapidly without relying on increased sales. The inability to improve sales in the short run is typical for a troubled company. Management, however, often devotes excessive energy to sales growth in the frantic hope that such action will cure all sins. Time would be better spent improving gross profit margins and reducing expenses. Our hypothetical company has a gross profit percentage of 42.3.

A careful analysis of each product line, however, reveals that selective price increases can be made immediately on proprietary products without affecting volume.

Management believes that the salespeople would aggressively promote these more expensive products if their commission structure was improved. Price increases are estimated to generate a sales increase of $536,000, offset by increased commission expenses of $108,000. This decision alone, which can be promptly implemented, will contribute $428,000 to the pretax profit of company XYZ. In addition, a minor change in freight policy will offset certain costs. The company owns a luxury vehicle which it can sell to generate some revenue and

TABLE 3-2
Company XYZ
Balance Sheet
For Fiscal Year Ending _____
($000)

Assets	
Cash	$ (1,500)
Accounts receivable	871,800
Inventory	702,700
Other	270,900
Total current assets	1,843,900
Property, plant, and equipment	600,200
Allowance for depreciation	262,800
Net fixed assets	337,400
Other assets	2,200
Total assets	$2,183,500
Liabilities and Stockholders' Equity	
Accounts payable	$ 873,000
Loans payable	781,700
Current portion of long-term debt	103,600
Taxes payable	5,700
Total current liabilities	1,764,000
Notes payable	242,700
Stockholder loans payable	159,400
Total long-term debt	402,100
Total liabilities	2,166,100
Capital stock	37,100
Retained earnings	(19,700)
Total stockholders' equity	17,400
Total liabilities and equity	$2,183,500

avoid future operating expenses in this area. Certain selling, general, and administrative costs can be reduced immediately to improve potential net income.

The company had previously absorbed the freight cost for products ordered at a given volume. By raising the volume level eligible for this benefit, the company can reduce the cost of sales by $93,000, assuming that customers do not raise or lower their ordering patterns.

It had been the policy of the company to place large institutional ads in a major magazine three times a year. These ads are considered unnecessary in the company's current condition, and their cancellation results in a savings of $69,000.

The company has reviewed its policies and procedures related to travel and entertainment. Trips to the Far East are immediately limited to one per year, resulting in a savings of $35,000. The balance of the savings in the travel and entertainment category, $26,000, comes from better control over trucking and changes in policies related to automobiles and air flight. All first-class flights are eliminated, and employees are required to take advantage of the special airline rates that are now quite prevalent.

Management also believes it could reduce staffing in the sales department by one service person, resulting in a savings of $25,000. The company luxury vehicle could be sold at its net cost; the annual cost of maintenance and insurance, totalling $8,000, will therefore be saved.

In the general and administrative area, management determines that two executive positions could be consolidated, resulting in a net savings of $23,000. During troubled times there are often opportunities to consolidate positions at the upper end of the organizational hierarchy, where salaries and benefits are highest. Decisions of this kind, by their very nature, can only be made by the top executive.

A quick review of the balance sheet reveals that an overdraft position exists on the company's books, although because of the float, an overdraft has not yet been generated at the

bank. The working capital (current assets less current liabilities) is only $78,900. The working capital ratio is 1.05, significantly less than the minimum acceptable level of 1.5 for this type of business. The total debt/equity ratio, which the lenders would like to see at 1.5 to feel comfortable, is an astronomical 12.5! Inventory turnover, which should be at 6.0 to 1, is only 4.7 to 1. We see before us a troubled company.

The company must take immediate steps to control cash, which will be discussed in detail in Chapter 6. Improving profits in the long run improves the balance sheet, but the balance sheet items must be reviewed and direct action taken in the short run.

SHORT-TERM ACTION PLAN

After many agonizing meetings, management is able to take immediate steps to generate a net improvement of $707,000 and realize a profit before interest and taxes of $641,000. These steps involved the following:

Selective price increases and changes in the sales commission structure	$ 536,000
Increased commissions	(108,000)
Changes in the policy on prepaid freight	93,000
Reduction in advertising costs	69,000
Changes in travel and entertainment policies and reduction of travel	61,000
Salary reductions—selling	25,000
Sale of luxury vehicle (net benefit including maintenance and insurance)	8,000
Salary reductions—general and administrative	23,000
Net improvement	$ 707,000

These short-range steps alone dramatically change the potential profit picture. The revised profit and loss statement is shown in Table 3-3.

The $707,000 is further enhanced by a reduction in debt and hence in the interest expense for the year. This improved per-

TABLE 3-3
Company XYZ
Revised Profit and Loss

Sales	$6,248,000
Cost of sales	3,204,000
Gross profit	3,044,000
Selling expense	1,693,000
General and administrative expense	722,000
Total operating expense	2,415,000
Other income	12,000
Profit before taxes and interest	$ 641,000

formance actually enables the company one year later to reduce its interest rate significantly and to obtain a regular revolving line of credit.

As the company phases into this short-term plan, it needs the cooperation of its existing lenders and creditors. Weaker staff people are terminated, the president and executive vice president take voluntary salary reductions, and the key vendors agree to extend credit in the usual manner.

LONG-TERM PLAN

Simultaneously, the company embarks on a longer-term program that will yield even greater savings in the second year. These included:

- A distribution analysis and warehouse location study to lower freight cost from $563,000 to $310,000—a savings of $253,000
- An improved inventory management system to increase inventory turnover to 6.0 and cash flow by $170,000
- A change in sales methods to reduce selling expenses by $100,000
- The introduction of a unique product to increase sales by over $1,000,000
- The sale of an unprofitable subsidiary

Other intangible improvements involve upgrading the accounting and management reporting systems and significantly modifying the company's employee benefits program.

I have seen other companies in a similar situation end up filing a Chapter XI!

Unfortunately, some companies cannot solve their problem without the infusion of outside funds and/or the restructuring of their debt. Problems of this nature will be discussed more fully in Chapter 4.

MAXIMIZING INTERNAL CASH FLOW

The whole area of maximization of internal cash flow is so important that some of the more common sources of funds require further discussion:

Sale of Inventories. During the energy crisis, a major recreational vehicle manufacturer obtained millions of dollars by completing a bulk sale for a finished product that was virtually unsellable through its normal channels of distribution. Many companies have taken their slow-moving products and sold them at significant discounts, at times even below cost. Sometimes vendors will take back merchandise, thereby enabling a company to reduce payables and increase credit. Providing attractive price breaks for high-volume sales can often be an effective way to generate cash.

Your company should prepare a complete detailed listing of its inventory, showing units, cost value, and current sales value. Review each item to determine whether your company should retain the same price level or develop selling incentives. Remember, cash is king. If inventory is not secured currently, you may be able to obtain an inventory loan on a short-term basis.

Reduction of the Collection Cycle. Many companies lack both an aggressive collection policy and aggressive people to enforce the collections. The men or women running your collection function must be ironclad and inner-directed—able to absorb the "slings and arrows" of your customers and to stop any delay tactics before they get out of hand. If your collection personnel are not tough enough, replace them right away. This is not the job for "nice people." Once the news is out that a company is in trouble, the receivables begin to age and debts are challenged. Again, you must make a complete listing of all your receivables, ranking their balances from high to low. Individuals must be assigned specific accounts and directed to report back promptly on their results. When a vendor refuses to pay a bill, his or her reasons must be clearly spelled out (reasons may include poor financial condition, an incorrect bill, displeasure with a product or service, incomplete documentation, etc.). If the problem is related to accounting, the company must get to the customer and resolve the problem on the spot. If the customer is unhappy with a product or service, determine if the reasons are valid, then either settle, correct the problem, or take back the merchandise. If the customer is in poor financial condition, check financial statements to verify this, take back available merchandise, threaten to talk to the customer's bank, and/or try to collateralize the receivable. If all else fails, the president must be prepared to contact the vendor personally and to take the necessary action to get the money.

These matters will be reviewed at the weekly cash-flow meeting, which will be discussed in Chapter 6.

Sale of Fixed Assets. A detailed inventory of all assets should be taken carefully, showing the current market value of the assets net of any existing debt. Often idle pieces of real estate, worth significantly more than book value, are available. If the company owns an active plant that must remain in operation, a sale and leaseback may provide much-needed funds. If a facilities consolidation is being considered, try subleasing or selling off the unused space. The analysis of equipment may reveal machines no longer in use that have excellent market value. If at all possible, try to avoid selling to the many mass liquidators who will approach you once they hear of your problem.

Consolidations and Shutdown of Facilities. Sometimes the largest benefits are realized by shutting down facilities. This is often a painful decision because it involves termination and/or relocation of many people. Moreover, psychologically, we have many "sunk cost" dollars tied up in the facility. Dollars spent in the past are gone. They will never return. Management must ignore them completely and look toward the reduction of future costs. Maintaining excess capacity during a crisis is too costly. Sometimes a facility can be sublet; often an equitable termination agreement can be made with the landlord; and sometimes it is cheaper to maintain the lease and eliminate all other costs related to the facility.

It is critical to get the company into the smallest space needed to implement the new plan of action. Of course, geography and management control are considerations that will play a vital part in any final decisions.

Proper Management of Accounts Payable. Solving the accounts payable problem is a primary key to survival. We are dealing, however, with a two-edged sword. On the one hand, we need the support of our vendors to stay in business; on the other hand, we can't afford to pay them in a timely manner. In facing a payables dilemma, management often "drags" vendors, hoping they won't notice, neglecting to inform them that a financial problem exists.

Chapter 2 discussed how to determine the unsecured creditor's exposure. Remember, the greater the potential loss, the more leverage you may have in getting creditor support. After you have created the short-term action plan discussed earlier in this section and have established a short-term cash flow for the "critical period before turnaround," it will become clear what type of support you will need.

First, obtain a detailed payables run and get the current aging for each vendor. Identify those vendors whom you need to stay in business, those who are currently dormant, and those who can be easily replaced by alternative sources of supply. In addition, be alert to adverse vendor relationships that may already exist. If they are not handled properly, you could find yourself facing involuntary bankruptcy. Also, watch for small vendors whom *you* may put into bankruptcy by not paying them. They, too, may feel it essential to take strong legal action against your company.

Second, develop a plan of attack. Know specifically what your plans are for each vendor. Then have the appropriate personnel in your company meet with the vendor to work out the agreement. This is a tedious process, but it will provide enormous benefits. Most important, once an agreement has been reached, honor it; this is essential. Here is a partial list of arrangements that can be made:

- Extension of credit over a longer period (for example, 60 to 90 days).
- Freezing of existing debt, or shorter credit extension (or COD) on new debt.
- Conversion of all or a portion of the debt to a long-term note, with a new credit program on future debt.
- Conversion of all or part of the debt to equity.
- Cancellation of a portion of the debt in return for prompt payment. (This should only be considered in the more acute situations.)
- Where appropriate, a joint marketing program to sell your product in return for "off-the-top" debt repayment.
- Where appropriate, return of merchandise for debt reduction.

Third, monitor your commitments at the highest level and make certain they are honored.

Identification of Areas for Immediate Revenue Increase. This is an area requiring a high level of creativity. Sometimes the best short-term opportunities are at your doorstep.

Probably the most obvious source is *price increases*. At this point, you must have a "heart-to-heart" with your sales and marketing people. Minor and well-selected price increases can work wonders. When you are making the pricing decisions, keep in mind that profit margins and cash flow are more important than sales growth. Next, see if you can sell your existing products (possibly with some minor modifications) to new markets. Here are a few examples:

- A manufacturer of cans for potato chips found that the cans could also hold three tennis balls.
- During the energy crisis, a recreational vehicle manufacturer sold trailers as mobile offices and built portable outhouses.
- A distributor of tapes discovered that by putting the customer's name on the tapes, a substantial price increase could be justified and new customers identified.
- A manufacturer of total solar-system packages learned that more revenue and a higher rate of profitability could be generated by selling only the energy control unit to previous competitors who manufactured and/or distributed collectors.
- A distributor of wood products found a ready, more profitable market in home building than in the commercial construction industry on which the company had previously focused.

Sometimes existing sources of business can generate additional revenue by supplying auxiliary products or services. Most real estate lenders, for example, augment their revenue by offering insurance to their customers. Manufacturers of recreational vehicles offer options such as fire extinguishers, flashlights, and beverage holders. Some manufacturers of systems offer consulting services to their customers for a fee. I even know of a manufacturer of manhole covers who sold molds to artists, who in turn incorporated them in their metal sculptures. The opportunities, of course, are different for each type of business, but these innovations may suggest other possibilities to you.

Identification of Areas for Cost Reduction. This is such a broad area that a proper discussion of cost reduction deserves a whole book itself. The best approach is to develop a general checklist by major areas such as shown here:

ORGANIZATION

- Can the number of management positions be reduced through consolidation of functions?
- Can salary reductions be effectively implemented for some positions?
- Can a freeze or tight approval procedure be implemented for all new personnel?
- Are there economies in centralizing or decentralizing certain functions?
- Is there duplication of effort or responsibility?
- Would across-the-board personnel cost reductions work in the short run?
- Can certain service departments be eliminated?

FINANCE, ACCOUNTING, AND MANAGEMENT REPORTING

- Can certain unnecessary reports and their related costs of preparation be eliminated?
- Is cash being spent to minimize the overall cost of money?
- Is the cash management function centralized to ensure maximum utilization of scarce funds?
- Can the costs related to audit and tax work be reduced?
- Is the cost accounting sufficient to identify unprofitable products and departments so that effective action can be taken?
- Can the flow of paperwork be reduced?
- Can a lid be put on any capital expenditures?

MARKETING AND SALES

- Can policies be implemented to reduce the travel and entertainment expenditures incurred by existing personnel?
- Can a freeze be put on advertising commitments? Can the company get out of commitments that have already been made?
- Can the method of selling be reorganized—e.g., by territory or by function—to reduce the number of personnel?
- Can the commission structure be modified to reduce expenses?
- Are there opportunities for personnel reductions and outside consultation reductions in the marketing area?
- Can cost reductions be realized by altering the marketing approach (e.g., by using brokers, direct mail, or agents)?
- Is there excessive discounting of products?

DISTRIBUTION

- Can distribution changes be made to reduce cost (e.g., by using trucks, planes, or company transports)?
- Can personnel reductions be made in the distribution area?
- Is the paperwork excessive?
- Are warehouses and related facilities properly located for minimal cost?
- Is inventory kept too high to offset a poor distribution control system?

MANUFACTURING

- Has the bill of materials been recently reviewed to ensure proper products are purchased on the best terms?
- Can purchasing be simplified and personnel reductions implemented?
- Has the direct labor cost area been reviewed to improve work routing and to achieve cost reductions?

- Are there too many high-priced direct labor personnel in relation to existing needs? Is there excess supervision?
- Have general overhead expenses such as insurance and engineering been recently evaluated?
- Can manufacturing's square footage be reduced and the new available space be sold or leased?

The questions can go on and on. This is one area where qualified management consultants can often save you a great deal of money.

At this stage you have bought time and have used it to establish short-term viability. You now have the breathing space necessary to develop a more comprehensive strategy supported by a workable business plan.

Corporate Strategy and Business Plan

Chapter **4**

The precise format for a business plan and the corporate strategy necessary for its creation are unique for each company and for each situation. In most cases, the plan probably would include but not be limited to the following:

1. A summary of the financial requirements
2. A discussion of the company—its history, type of business, and facilities
3. The management and organization structure and an analysis of capabilities
4. A discussion of the recent losses and the company's response
5. The industry outlook
6. Corporate strategy
7. Forecast assumptions
8. Forecast schedules

SUMMARY OF FINANCIAL REQUIREMENTS

This section of the business plan is normally a brief statement of:

1. What the company is seeking based on its internal capabilities

57

2. The industry outlook
3. The financial assumptions it has made as well as the pro forma profit and loss, balance sheet, and cash-flow statements derived from those assumptions

The statement would quantify the amount, timing, and type of funding desired. The types of funding could include: equity, convertible debt, long-term debt, revolving lines of credit, and inventory and accounts receivable loans.

A brief discussion would then follow, explaining how the new injection of funds would be utilized to put the company on a solid footing.

THE COMPANY

This section of the business plan normally tells the reader how long the company has been in business and provides historical and financial data showing, at a minimum, sales and profits. Its purpose is to demonstrate that the business was well managed prior to the crisis. A discussion of the major source of revenue (customer profile) generally follows. Where appropriate, certain intangible benefits should be highlighted, such as:

- Market position
- Unique programs
- Special arrangements
- Distribution network
- Proprietary products
- Quality of products or services and reputation
- Brand name identification

It is also important to describe the current facilities: type of structure, square footage, and utilization of space.

If the company is completely or partially unionized or if special restrictive agreements exist, these must be identified and explained.

Generally, a brief description of how the company conducts its business is included in this section.

MANAGEMENT AND ORGANIZATION

This section of the business plan should include an overall organization chart showing the reporting relationships between top-, middle-, and lower-management levels. A brief description of the major executive positions, including responsibility, authority, and qualifications, is useful to the potential investor. This should be followed by a discussion related to the organizational philosophy of the company: centralization vs. decentralization, product line vs. functional, project vs. process.

Particular emphasis should be given to the experience, longevity, and talent of the key personnel. Keep in mind that potential investors are concerned about the ability of management to effectively utilize the new funding they will be providing. After all, if the existing management was in place when the company got into trouble, why should investors now believe this same management will get the company out of trouble? In response to this last question, the next section is absolutely essential to a good business plan.

RECENT LOSSES AND THE COMPANY'S RESPONSE

This is a difficult section of the business plan to write because it will demonstrate how well you, as management, understand why you got into trouble. Are your problems due only to outside forces in the economy? Did management inadequacies play a great part in creating the financial problem? The causes of your losses must not only be *identified* but be *quantified*. The potential investors must believe that the causes of your losses were "one-time" occurrences and that the root of the problem has been corrected. Unfortunately, if your company has a poor accounting and management reporting system, it will have great difficulty developing the information needed for this section of the business plan.

The first step is to identify the *external* causes of the problem. These may include:

- The energy crisis
- A slowdown in the economy
- Tight money markets
- Heavy competition from major companies
- Negative government regulation
- Fires, floods, and other damage to key facilities
- Unusually bad weather
- Shortage of supply of key raw material
- Certain key customers experiencing their own financial crises
- Nationalization of overseas facilities
- Currency-exchange problems

It is all too easy to blame *all* the problems on causes such as the above. However, once these sources of loss are quantified carefully, two major questions usually remain unanswered:

1. What were the causes of the remaining losses?
2. Was the externally caused loss effectively handled and kept to a minimum?

The next step, therefore, is to identify the *internal* causes of the problem, such as:

- Poor financial controls
- Incorrect marketing decisions to sell a particular product
- Premature corporate expansion
- Excessive management
- Competence deficiencies in certain key functions
- Quality control problems
- Failure to control pricing

- Lack of inventory control
- Slow collections
- Shutdowns, out-of-stock conditions, and erratic production
- Communication problems in the organization
- Out-of-control selling expenses and general and administrative expenses
- Failure to respond promptly to the external causes once they were identified

The list is endless, but it is important to identify clearly the significant causes of the loss in order to take the next step: *quantification.*

A simple example of the quantification analysis is shown in Table 4-1.

TABLE 4-1
ABC Company
Analysis of Losses for
Fiscal ____

Normal Profit	$ 2,600,000
External Problems	
Bad weather in Northeast, resulting in 30-day shutdown of New Jersey plant	(850,000)
Exchange losses between the yen and dollar	(550,000)
Increase in interest from the planned rate of X% to Y% due to tight money market	(160,000)
Shutdown of production line due to supply shortage in Far East.	(790,000)
Expected profit performance due to external problems	$250,000
Internal Problems	
Poor purchasing, resulting in obsolete inventory write-offs	(430,000)
Purchasing of raw material in excess of planned standard	(480,000)
Collection problems resulting in a need to increase the bad-debt reserve	(340,000)
Overstaffing in general and administration and selling in relation to plan	$(250,000)
Actual Reported Losses for Fiscal Year	$(1,250,000)

By a careful review of Table 4-1, the potential investor now knows that $2,350,000 in losses were created by external causes. The external causes should be evaluated to see if they apply for the coming year. The bad weather in the northeastern part of the United States caused a shutdown for the first time in the company's history and is unlikely to occur in the near future at that level of severity; exchange losses are expected to be less severe, resulting in a loss of about $280,000; interest is expected to remain at X percent, resulting in a loss of $160,000; and the supply problem in the Far East has been corrected. If all other factors remain the same, the potential loss from external causes is expected to be reduced from $2,350,000 to $440,000. This $1,910,000 improvement alone would generate a profit (at the same volume level) of $660,000, even if the internal problems are not corrected.

The final task is to show how the company plans to correct the past internal problems which increased losses by $1,500,000:

New purchasing policies are implemented and personnel are upgraded.	$910,000
An inventory management system is installed to ensure that obsolete items are more rapidly identified and to provide for optional-level dollar investment in inventory.	$660,000
A system for qualifying customers is instituted. Credit limits are established for customers. A more aggressive collection program is established. Personnel upgrading is completed.	$340,000
A reduction of personnel in selling and general and administration is completed.	$250,000
	$2,160,000

All other factors being the same, the company can expect a profit of $2,160,000 next year based on a flat sales year. This benefit would be either increased or decreased in relation to next year's sales forecast.

Additional savings that might also be realized for next year will be covered in the section on corporate strategy.

THE INDUSTRY OUTLOOK

This section of the business plan is designed to give external support to your analysis and conclusions regarding the external causes of the problem (discussed in the previous section). Consider the case of a company which is located in city X and tied to the construction industry, to capital spending, and to the related long-term money markets. To bolster its position, the company can quote journals and periodicals put out by the construction industry. It can quote the City X Economic Bulletin on the subject of new permits issued. An evaluation by respected investment counseling services and economic outlook studies by some of the larger financial institutions may also be invaluable in supporting the company's assumptions about the future. Using the above information plus known facts about itself, the company can construct a picture of its outlook for next year and, in less detail, for two to four more years into the future.

Properly written, this section of the business plan can reassure potential investors that someone besides the management of the company agrees with the industry outlook. It can also demonstrate that the company has an accurate picture of its industry, community, and existing market position.

CORPORATE STRATEGY

Many fine books have been written on this subject. Potential investors now understand the nature of your company, how you are organized, what created your financial problem, how you corrected that problem, and what the overall industry outlook appears to be. This section of the business plan will tell them how the company will be operated in the short term and over the next few years. The corporate strategy should be defined clearly and should avoid platitudes such as "we will be the best company in our industry."

You may find it helpful to reflect on alternative types of overall strategies available to a business. One or more may be applicable to your own company.

1. **Survival.**   Run the company in its present form. Maintain the same products and markets.
2. **New markets.**   Find new types of customers or locate customers in new geographical areas, including overseas. Maintain the same product.
3. **New products.**   Market new products to either existing or new customers.
4. **Product integration.**   This can be either forward or backward integration. Produce many of the raw materials that go into the finished product to reduce overall cost or, conversely, purchase subcomponents that were previously being manufactured for you by others.
5. **Abandonment.**   Consider vacating certain facilities, selling certain unprofitable subsidiaries, or eliminating an entire product line.
6. **Cost reduction.**   Introduce an austerity program resulting in personnel terminations and compensation reductions. Implement various programs to reduce non-personnel-related expenses. Improve the efficiency of production.
7. **New businesses.**   Establish new businesses through acquisition and merger, inside or outside the United States.
8. **Size reduction.**   Take the steps necessary to create a smaller but profitable business.
9. **Sales.**   Change the method of selling your product through licensing, franchising, sales representation, or telephone selling.
10. **Distribution.**   Change the method of distribution of product. Consider the use of trucks, railroads, and airlines, and the use of drop shipments.

FORECAST ASSUMPTIONS AND SCHEDULES

Before you develop the financial forecast schedules which include, at a minimum, balance sheet, cash-flow, and profit and loss statements, it is necessary to record a comprehensive list of assumptions from which the forecasts will be developed. These assumptions are the road map that will explain the basis for each number in the financial forecasts. They will enable the readers to judge for themselves the reasonableness of the forecasts. *This is the heart of the analysis.* It is here that the sophisticated reader finds out whether management knows what it is doing financially.

The actual pro forma forecasts depend on factors like the structure of the company, the kinds of businesses it operates, and the number of subsidiaries. As a general rule, forecasts are made on a monthly basis for the first year, on a quarterly basis for the second and possibly third year, and on an annual basis for all planning horizons in excess of three years.

Normally any planning beyond three years has a large element of "blue sky" speculation and is usually inaccurate. If, however, you are asking a bank for a five-year loan, the bank may want the planning horizon to cover the entire length of the loan period, thereby demonstrating the company's ability to service its debt commitment.

Let us now look carefully at the type of information included in the forecast assumptions (Exhibit 4-1). The first statement discusses the time horizon and frequency of the plan by year. The second statement provides the support for the sales forecast. (The company produces a product for an independent network, sells the product to its own outlets, and generates sales from a separate subsidiary.) Growth rates are stated, as is the impact of the rate of inflation. Plans for expansion or contraction are then summarized for each division by facility. Plant capacity and sales forecasts are discussed to ensure that the units projected are reasonable in terms of product capability.

EXHIBIT 4-1
Forecast Assumptions

1. The forecast is for a five-year (5-year) period beginning May 1, 1979, and ending April 30, 1984. Financial information in the forecast is presented quarterly for the fiscal years 1980, 1981, and 1982, and annually for the fiscal years 1983 and 1984.
2. Sales forecast for fiscal 1980 were estimated by management. They are based upon the current requirements and trends of our existing network and on a detailed analysis of our current product requirements of our factory-owned operating outlets, and they have been adjusted to reflect actual sales for the first six (6) months of fiscal 1980. For the fiscal years beginning May 1, 1980, and ending April 30, 1984, based upon past trends and the current economic climate, it was estimated conservatively that of the dollar growth forecast, six (6) percent would be the result of inflation, while four (4) percent would represent true growth. No additional expansion or opening of new facilities at the outlet or manufacturing levels are contemplated in the forecast.

   Sales forecast for the three divisions of ABC consisted of the following (in thousands of dollars):

Fiscal Years Ending April 30th	ABC Dealer Network	ABC Distribution Outlet	XYZ Subsidiaries	Total
1980	$26,390	$45,442	$23,753	$ 95,585
1981	41,532	47,266	26,129	114,927
1982	45,707	51,971	28,742	126,420
1983	50,277	57,168	31,616	139,061
1984	55,305	62,885	34,778	152,968

The divisions of ABC Industries presently consist of the following:

ABC Manufacturing

a. Plant A   Operating
b. Plant B   Operating
c. Plant C   Idle
d. Plant D   Idle
e. Plant E   Idle

While management intends to sell and/or sublease the idle facilities, their carrying cost has been provided for in the forecast for each of the five years.

EXHIBIT 4-1
Forecast Assumptions (*continued*)

XYZ Manufacturing

a. Plant F, Location A   Operating
b. Plant G, Location B   Operating

The production of ABC products required for their independent network and outlets will be scheduled for approximately sixty (60) percent at Plant A and forty (40) percent at Plant B. The forecast would require production ranging from a low of $7\frac{1}{2}$ units to a high of 20 units per day during fiscal 1980, and from $10\frac{1}{2}$ to 26 units per day for fiscal 1984. Of this, Plant A's production would be maximized at 16 units per day while Plant B's production would be maximized at $10\frac{1}{2}$ units. The product lines average the following equivalent units:

a. Type 1   1 unit
b. Type 2 $\frac{3}{5}$ of 1 unit
c. Type 3 $\frac{1}{4}$ of 1 unit
d. Type 4 $\frac{1}{2}$ of 1 unit

Based on our present estimate of market requirements, Plant A and Plant B have ample capacity to handle ABC's needs as forecast.

XYZ's production is anticipated to handle sixty (60) percent at Plant F and forty (40) percent at Plant G.

The forecast, while taking into consideration special payment arrangements made with automotive companies, does not include the special programs entered into with MNO Motors.

3. Receivables have been estimated to be collectible in a manner which reflects our historical experience and current collection policies:

ABC Manufacturing

a. 50%   Current month
b. 40%   30 to 60 days
c. 10%   60 to 90 days

XYZ Manufacturing

a. Independent outlets:
   (1) 50%   Current Month
   (2) 50%   30 to 60 days
b. Outlet sales in month of sale

4. Manufacturing inventories have been projected to flow in the following manner:
   a. Material purchased 30 days prior to production
   b. Production 30 days prior to sale
   c. Purchases of chassis have been included in inventories based on anticipated delivery and needs which approximate 30 days prior to sale

(*continued*)

EXHIBIT 4-1
Forecast Assumptions (continued)

5. Accounts payable have been estimated to be maintained on a 60-day basis for ABC and 45 to 60 days for XYZ. In some instances they are below that level in order to provide for price negotiation. During fiscal 1984, scheduled payments also include approximately $100,000 for special arrangements that may be required.

6. Repurchase losses have been provided for by ABC in the forecast for fiscal 1984 in the following manner:
   a. $100,000 cash outlay in the current month
   b. $80,000 increase in inventory in the current month
   c. $70,000 resale in the following month
   d. $30,000 loss included in the manufacturing variances in each month from August 1979 through April 1980

   It is not anticipated that subsequent to fiscal 1984 ABC will experience any additional repurchase losses because of the new buy-back agreements negotiated with the lending institutions.

   No repurchase losses were forecast for XYZ because it is not their policy to enter into any buy-back arrangements with finance companies.

7. ABC Manufacturing includes sales at wholesale to factory-owned outlets. In the forecast, these sales totalled the following (in thousands of dollars):

a. Fiscal 1980	$20,569
b. Fiscal 1981	23,279
c. Fiscal 1982	25,603
d. Fiscal 1983	28,154
e. Fiscal 1984	30,970

   These sales have been eliminated in the consolidated profit and loss statements. The profit in inventories has been eliminated in the consolidated balance sheets.

   For forecasting purposes, it was not anticipated that there would be any intercompany shipments of product between ABC and XYZ.

   Gross profits on location sales were estimated at the following: ABC products, twelve (12) percent; used products, eighteen (18) percent; parts and accessories, twenty-four (24) percent.

   Other revenue and expenses were computed by an analysis of each individual location. Finance income was not forecast for the Eastern outlets because of the high current financing rates. Finance income will increase if the interest rates are reduced during the forecast years.

8. On November 1, 1979, the company renegotiated its loan agreement with its principal bank. This revision, among other things, extended

EXHIBIT 4-1
Forecast Assumptions (continued)

the maturity of X_1 million of loans to April 30, 1981. The total loan bears interest at 130 percent of the prime bank rate which, at the time of execution of the agreement, was X_2 percent. The remaining short-term borrowing of $_____$, together with accrued interest of I percent, was extended as a revolving credit line. This credit line shall bear interest at the rate of one (1) percent above the prime bank rate and is to be paid quarterly, or at the maturity of the loan. In addition, the agreement provided for additional borrowings of X_3 million bearing interest at one (1) percent above prime. This X_3 million is partially secured by certain parcels of real estate. Of the above loan, $700,000 is payable in weekly installments of $100,000 plus interest beginning November 1, 1979. The remaining balance will mature on April 30, 1981. Although the X_4 million bank loan matures on April 30, 1981, and becomes a short-term obligation on May 1, 1980, for the purpose of this forecast, it has been treated as a long-term obligation until its forecast liquidation, which is as follows:

Payment made during quarter ending 7/31/78	$ 1,662,000
Payment made during quarter ending 4/30/79	3,500,000
Payment made during year ending 4/30/80	4,000,000
Payment made during year ending 4/30/81	8,503,000
Total long-term bank debt	$17,665,000

All interest which was forecast to be deferred has been treated as an increase in accrued liabilities (short-term obligation).

9. On April 30, 1979, the company had a net operating loss carry-forward for U.S. federal income tax purposes of approximately $X million that would expire in 1984. The company files a consolidated tax return for all its U.S.-based companies. For the purposes of this forecast, the following income tax rates were used:

U.S. federal income taxes	48%
Foreign income taxes	42%
State income or franchise taxes based on income	7½%

The net operating loss carry-forward was used in the forecast on net income earned by ABC, excluding XYZ.

The third statement explains the collection rate for each division. This assumption is critical to the future cash flow and hence to the borrowing needs of the company.

The fourth statement deals with the calculation of inventory levels. Since this company manufactures products, the assumptions related to purchasing and production become quite critical. If inventory turnover can be increased and overall inventory levels lowered, then in relation to sales, cash flow is enhanced.

The fifth statement discusses the rate at which disbursements will be made. The longer creditors can be extended without jeopardizing the flow of product or services, the better the cash flow. It is often better to sacrifice the purchase discounts and maximize the extension of credit when a company is in difficulty.

Statement six relates to repurchase losses, which are unique to this industry. Under the repurchase agreements, the ABC Company may be required to buy back finished inventory from certain lending institutions should an independent dealer go out of business.

Because there are intercompany sales, statement seven is necessary to explain their nature and the amounts to be eliminated.

Statement eight outlines the debt structuring with the company's existing financial institution, including payment commitments, conversion of debt from short to long term, deferral of interest, and so on.

The ninth assumption points out the availability of a net operating loss carry-forward which could have important future value in improving cash flow.

These assumptions provide the mathematical framework for the balance sheet, profit and loss, and cash-flow forecasts. If these assumptions seem reasonable to you, then study the logical financial outcome in Tables 4-2 to 4-4.

TABLE 4-2

ABC Industries, Inc. and Subsidiaries

Consolidated Balance Sheet

($000)

	As at							
	July 31, 1979	Oct. 31, 1979	Jan. 31, 1980	Apr. 30, 1980	July 31, 1980	Oct. 31, 1980	Jan. 31, 1981	Apr. 30, 1981
Assets								
Cash	$ 652	$ 485	$(2,831)	$(1,487)	$ 1,407	$ 1,345	$ 357	$ 519
Accounts receivable—net	4,111	3,416	4,105	6,053	5,584	2,882	4,786	8,431
Inventories	21,823	19,486	21,408	19,631	17,045	18,253	22,463	20,586
Others	904	1,261	1,093	957	1,093	1,030	980	930
Total noncash	26,838	24,163	26,606	26,641	23,722	22,165	28,229	29,947
Total current	27,490	24,648	23,775	25,154	25,129	23,510	28,586	30,466
Property, plant, and equipment	18,831	19,322	19,525	19,675	19,708	19,742	19,778	19,814
Allowance for accumulative depreciation	(2,948)	(3,462)	(3,976)	(4,490)	(5,049)	(5,608)	(6,168)	(6,728)
Net fixed assets	15,883	15,860	15,549	15,185	14,659	14,134	13,610	13,086
Investments and other	2,675	3,319	3,365	3,357	3,331	3,324	3,315	3,283
Total assets	$46,048	$43,827	$42,689	$43,696	$43,119	$40,968	$45,511	$46,835
Liabilities and Stockholders' Equity								
Accounts payable	$ 7,065	$ 5,081	$ 5,825	$ 5,774	$ 5,967	$ 5,039	$ 6,634	$ 8,271
Accrued liabilities	1,504	1,510	1,788	2,196	1,018	960	1,283	1,263
Notes payable—unsecured	16,629	8,122	8,791	7,710	5,000	5,000	6,500	3,200
Notes payable—secured	14,529	9,070	8,747	8,312	8,444	7,609	8,843	8,522

TABLE 4-2 (*Continued*)
ABC Industries, Inc. and Subsidiaries
Consolidated Balance Sheet
($000)

	As at							
	July 31, 1979	Oct. 31, 1979	Jan. 31, 1980	Apr. 30, 1980	July 31, 1980	Oct. 31, 1980	Jan. 31, 1981	Apr. 30, 1981
Accrued income taxes	19	(97)	(230)	—	605	549	402	848
Current installment—long-term debt	1,739	1,734	1,725	1,723	723	721	721	721
Total current liabilities	41,485	25,420	26,646	25,715	21,757	19,878	24,383	22,825
Long-term debt	3,778	20,606	20,441	20,275	21,120	20,867	20,711	20,554
Deferred taxes	531	531	531	531	531	531	531	531
Total long-term debt	4,309	21,137	20,972	20,806	21,651	21,398	21,242	21,085
Total equity	254	(2,730)	(4,929)	(2,825)	(289)	(308)	(114)	2,925
Total liabilities and equity	$46,048	$43,827	$42,689	$43,696	$43,119	$40,968	$45,511	$46,835

72

TABLE 4-3
ABC Industries, Inc. and Subsidiaries
Consolidated Statement of Earnings (Loss)
($000)

	Quarter Ending							
	July 31, 1979	Oct. 31, 1979	Jan. 31, 1980	Apr. 30, 1980	July 31, 1980	Oct. 31, 1980	Jan. 31, 1981	Apr. 30, 1981
Sales (net)	$23,753	$19,181	$18,981	$33,670	$35,885	$19,812	$22,001	$37,229
Cost of sales	20,781	17,516	16,866	27,044	28,315	15,959	17,878	29,355
Gross profit	2,972	1,665	2,115	6,626	7,570	3,853	4,123	7,874
Selling, administration, and other	3,200	3,320	3,072	2,952	3,150	2,790	2,833	3,204
Interest expense	1,173	1,211	1,141	1,172	1,053	941	971	958
Idle facility costs	144	144	144	107	107	107	107	107
Total expenses	4,517	4,675	4,357	4,231	4,310	3,838	3,911	4,269
Profit (loss) before tax	(1,545)	(3,010)	(2,242)	2,395	3,260	15	212	3,605
Income tax	325	(26)	(43)	291	724	34	18	566
Net after tax	$(1,870)	$(2,984)	$(2,199)	$ 2,104	$ 2,536	$ (19)	$ 194	$ 3,039

73

TABLE 4-4
ABC Industries, Inc. and Subsidiaries
Consolidated Cash Flow
($000)

	Quarter Ending						
	Oct. 31, 1979	Jan. 31, 1980	Apr. 30, 1980	July 31, 1980	Oct. 31, 1980	Jan. 31, 1981	Apr. 30, 1981
Cash at start	$ 652	$ 485	$(2,831)	$(1,487)	$1,407	$1,345	$ 357
Add:							
Pretax profit	(3,010)	(2,242)	2,395	3,260	15	212	3,605
Decrease current assets	2,675	—	—	2,919	1,557		
Increase current liabilities	—	1,359	—	—	—	4,652	
Depreciation	514	514	514	559	559	560	560
Long-term borrowing	16,994						
Reduction in investment	—	—	8	26	7	9	32
Total provided	17,825	116	86	5,277	3,545	6,778	4,554
Less:							
Fixed assets purchased	491	203	150	33	34	36	36
Investments made	644	46	35				
Increase current assets	—	2,443	1,132				1,718
Decrease current liabilities	15,949	—		3,563	1,823	6,064	2,004
Tax payments	90	90	90	119	90	165	120
Pay long-term debt	166	165	166	155	253	156	157
Total used	17,340	2,947	1,573	3,870	2,200	6,421	4,035
Cash at end	$ 485	$(2,831)	$(1,487)	$1,407	$1,345	$ 357	$ 519

It is most important for the reader to understand that the balance sheet, profit and loss, and cash-flow statements are integrated. This can be seen most clearly by studying the cash-flow statement for the quarter ending October 31, 1979. The cash at the start, $652,000, is shown on the July 31, 1979, balance sheet. The cash balance was reduced by $3,010,000, the pretax loss shown on the October 31, 1979, statement of earnings. Current assets exclusive of cash was $26,838,000 on July 31, 1979, and $24,163,000 on October 31, 1979: a decrease of $2,675,000, which is a source of cash. Depreciation, while it is recorded as an expense for profit and loss reporting, must be added back because it is in actuality a noncash item. Long-term debt increased from $3,778,000 in July 31, 1979, to $21,137,000. On October 31, 1979, there was an increase of $16,994,000. This increase can be observed on the balance sheet and is the single most important source of cash for that period. In total, the above sources provided an additional $17,825,000 in cash. Why, then, did the ABC Company show an ending cash balance on October 31, 1979, of only $485,000? The answer lies in further analysis of the pro forma balance sheet. The company utilized $491,000 to purchase fixed investments assets. Investments increased by $644,000, from $2,675,000 to $3,319,000. Current liabilities decreased from $41,485,000 to $25,420,000, or by $15,949,000. This is the major use of cash, to pay down current debt. In addition, the company used $90,000 for payment of taxes and $166,000 to pay down the long-term debt. In total, the above uses of funds total $17,340,000. The beginning cash was, therefore, increased by $17,825,000 and reduced by $17,340,000, resulting in a new cash balance of $485,000. This ties in precisely with the amount shown on the October 31, 1979, balance sheet.

I go through this exercise because I believe many executives today do not understand that they are looking at one financial statement and not three separate statements. All too often, the focus is on the profit and loss component, at the expense of the balance and cash-flow components.

Chapter 5

Other Options

In the first four chapters, we explored the techniques of buying time and using that time effectively. Our emphasis was on seeking internal solutions to the company's problems. We looked for ways to maximize internal cash flow and to develop operational programs to reduce costs and increase revenue. We learned how to develop a meaningful corporate strategy and business plan, working primarily with existing resources. Unfortunately, there are times when it is not possible to solve the problems of a company in crisis without outside assistance. The available solutions can take many forms. The most common are:

1. Restructuring of debt with your existing bank
2. Arranging for private placement
3. Selling the company
4. Making informal creditor arrangements
5. Seeking outside sources of long-term money
6. Replacing management

RESTRUCTURING OF DEBT WITH YOUR EXISTING BANK

Sometimes the best source of funds is within your existing bank. If the company is in serious financial straits, the bank may recognize that it will have to absorb a large loss if the company fails. In Chapter 2, for example, we determined that the unsecured creditors could lose close to $23 million if the company filed for bankruptcy. The financial institution recognizes that when this happens: (1) inventories lose much of their value (particularly those items in the raw and in-process states); (2) many receivables that were good on a going-concern basis suddenly become uncollectible; (3) items that previously had been sold are now being returned in great numbers by customers giving various reasons for the unacceptability of the finished product; and (4) contingent liabilities have a strange way of coming out of the woodwork in the form of claims not provided for in the financial statements, sometimes resulting in large law suits.

If banks or other financial institutions could be convinced that the company could be made viable by a restructuring of the debt, it might be good business for you to take that step. Sometimes the restructuring of debt can be combined with the sale of certain subsidiaries. Let us look at the illustrative problem in Table 5-1. We can observe that ABC Industries has a deficit of over $30 million and a horrendous, negative working capital. The company is, in fact, technically bankrupt. However, ABC proposes to transfer its nonoperating properties to the bank, to dispose of other assets, and to persuade its creditors to agree to settle for little more than 10¢ on the dollar. The result would reduce the deficit to a little over $23 million. The company then proposes a debt conversion of close to $26 million in return for the preferred stock of this publicly held company.

As shown on the pro forma balance sheet for ABC Industries, the remaining debt to the bank was $25,927,000, including accrued interest. Upon final debt restructuring, which involved conversion of this remaining debt to convertible preferred stock, the surviving entity had a net worth of $2,324,000. Upon restructuring, the surviving entity had the following balance sheet characteristics:

TABLE 5-1
ABC Industries, Inc.
Pro Forma Balance Sheet
As of _____
($000)

	Current Estimation	Step 1[1]	Step 2[2]	Total before Restructuring	Step 3[3]	Total after Restructuring
Current assets	$ 3,617	—	$ (300)	$ 3,317	—	$3,317
Fixed assets	799	—	—	799	—	799
Nonoperating property	1,831	$(1,081)	—	750	—	750
Other assets						
Total assets	6,247	(1,081)	(300)	4,866	—	4,866
Obligations to bank	25,927	(1,081)	850	25,696	$(25,696)	—
Other current liabilities	9,933	—	(8,000)	1,933	—	1,933
Reserve for ABC operations	350	—	—	350	—	350
Other liabilities and deferred credits	259	—	—	259	—	259
Net worth (deficit)	(30,222)	—	6,850	(23,372)	25,696	2,324
Total liabilities and equity	$ 6,247	$(1,081)	$ (300)	$ 4,866	—	$4,866

[1]Step 1: transfer nonoperating properties to bank.
[2]Step 2: settle with creditors and dispose of other assets.
[3]Step 3: Restructure.

Current ratio   1.89
Debt/equity ratio   1.09

This provided a reasonable basis for viability and internal growth.

Let us examine Table 5-1 in greater detail. The first column shows the current balance sheet position of ABC Industries. Current assets are $3,617,000 and total assets are $6,247,000. Obligations to the bank are $25,927,000, current liabilities total $9,933,000, and various miscellaneous liabilities equal $609,000. The company, therefore, shows a deficit on its books of $30,222,000. As a first step in the restructuring process (the second column), ABC Industries takes $1,081,000 of nonoperating property and transfers it to the bank in return for a like debt reduction. The second step (the third column) assumes a successful creditor settlement (either inside or outside a formal proceeding), wherein $8,000,000 of unsecured debt is settled for $850,000. Unfortunately, the company does not have the $850,000 to pay the creditors and must, therefore, borrow this amount from the bank. The impact of this settlement is to increase bank debt by $850,000 and to reduce current liabilities from $9,933,000 to $1,933,000. In addition, inventory worth $600,000 is sold for $300,000. The current asset account Inventory declines by $600,000 and the current asset account Cash increases by $300,000, resulting in a net current asset reduction of $300,000. This $300,000 shrinkage in current assets and the bank loan of $850,000, offset by the reduction in current liabilities of $8,000,000, improves the net worth by $6,850,000. At the conclusion of the first two steps, bank debt is nominally reduced to $25,696,000, but the deficit is now $23,372,000 rather than $30,222,000. The third and final step involves conversion of the debt into equity. The equity will be a new class of preferred stock, as described below. The $2,324,000 difference between the bank debt and the deficit before restructuring now becomes the new net worth after restructuring. In many situations the financial institution may wish to retain some debt and only convert a portion of the debt. The bank may also agree to convert debt to equity in stages, based upon mutually agreed-to performance parameters. Keep in mind that the financial institution will only be cooperative in this restructuring effort if:

- It sees no other way to collect its debt
- It calculates a greater loss by not cooperating
- It believes the restructured entity would be viable

In the restructuring plan the bank has a few opportunities to recoup should the company be successful in the future:

- The preferred stock can be converted to common stock and sold with the company's next public offering
- The preferred stock is given priority in case of liquidation
- The preferred stock can receive dividends

The primary characteristics of the final debt restructuring program are now discussed.

Form of the Preferred Stock. It is proposed that the bank be issued shares of preferred stock, a measure which has previously been authorized by ABC's shareholders. The stock would:

- Have a par value of $Y per share.
- Be nonvoting but carry voting rights on any proposed merger or acquisition.
- Be protected against dilution.
- Contain liquidation preference.
- Have noncumulative dividend rights. Payment of dividends would be deferred for six years. Dividends at that time, on full conversion, would be the lesser of 10 percent of pretax profits or some given dollar amount. Such payments would in no event result in a current ratio of less than 1.9. Furthermore, the company would be legally capable of making such payments.

Conversion Formula. It is proposed that the remaining bank debt be converted into X shares of preferred stock. All or part of the preferred stock in turn will be convertible into Z shares of common stock at any time at the bank's option.

Debt Cancellation. The program calls for the cancellation of all debt at the completion of the creditor composition. ABC believes that the elimination of all remaining bank debt is in the best interest of the company and the bank because:

- It maximizes the net worth of the surviving entity, a situation which should positively impact the stock value
- It maximizes the earnings per share at any point in time, a condition which should also positively impact the stock value
- It allows the surviving entity to be financially self-sufficient
- It is a necessary basis for future borrowings for a revolving line of credit

Liquidation Preference Rights. It is proposed that the preferred stock have a liquidation preference under the following formula:

- The first $M goes to the bank.
- The proceeds, up to $N, are allocated as follows: 75% to preferred shareholders, and 25% to common shareholders
- Remaining proceeds go to the bank up to par.

Rights Relating to Sale of Converted Securities. In order to enable the bank to sell in the open market the common stock it has converted, the company agrees to:

- Use its best efforts to obtain an underwriting at the bank's direction three years after the conversion rights become effective
- Provide the bank with piggyback rights on the next two public offerings subject to any limitation that may be set by the underwriters

It is interesting to note that in situations such as the above, banks sometimes come out quite well. In making its decision the bank must, of course, weigh the proposed debt to equity conversion against other alternatives.

Other options could also have been considered. The bank might have converted a large portion of the current debt to a long-term note under preferential interest rates and payment arrangements. It might have offered some outright debt cancellation in return for the company's agreement to sell a major asset (possibly a subsidiary) and transfer all proceeds to the bank. The bank might have converted the debt directly into common stock or into a new class of common stock. The bank could have required redemption rights on the preferred stock, which would require the company to repurchase the stock at specified prices under specified conditions. Consideration also could have been given to waiving or deferring interest over the critical period.

The options are many, and creative work in this area can save the company and reduce the bank's loss. Unfortunately, the alternative of debt restructuring is rarely considered because neither the management of the company nor its advisers know how to design and implement such an option. One executive in trouble said to me, "After spending so many years telling my bank how great our company was, how do I let them know that (1) we screwed up, (2) they will have to take a financial bath, and (3) I need them to forgive or convert our debt to bail us out?!" The answer is simple: "Ask."

ARRANGING FOR PRIVATE PLACEMENT

In a risk situation potential equity investors may see an opportunity to buy a position in the problem company at discount prices. The company can seek out groups of investors directly or through a private placement. The placement must state the purpose of the offering, the minimum purchase per investor, qualifications required of the potential investors, conditions precedent to purchase, restrictions imposed on the securities, the risk factors, access to company information, and registration rights. Shown in Exhibit 5-1 is a sample of a private placement memorandum. In this example, ABC Industries is traded publicly.

Let us examine the Private Placement Memorandum for ABC Industries in more detail. The first paragraphs emphasize that the information contained in the memorandum cannot be distributed without the company's consent. These restrictions in the dissemination of information are required by the Securities and Exchange Commission.

The paragraph entitled *The Offering* points out that shares are for investment only, with a minimum purchase of $100,000 per investor. This limits, for example, a $2,000,000 offer to a maximum of 20 investors.

The next paragraph, *Limitations of Offering,* sets forth the minimum financial capabilities of the investor in terms of net worth and net income. Then, *Use of Proceeds* states that the funds will be utilized as general working capital.

The section *Subscription Agreement and Escrow* describes the agreement to be signed for the purchase, explains all other costs, and describes how the funds will be delivered and exchanged for stock.

The next section, entitled *Restricted Securities,* informs the investor about the nature of the securities and emphasizes that shares purchased cannot be immediately sold. Under certain conditions, the investor can unilaterally sell his or her shares after a two-year holding period. In essense, this section reemphasizes that the purchase should be for investment only.

Risk Factors, though a brief section in this exhibit, is quite crucial. The investor must be fully informed about the risks inherent in the investment. Although it may scare off the less hardy investor, I suggest the list of risks be as exhuastive as possible.

In the *Access to Further Information* section, ABC Industries agrees to provide the investor with any additional information needed to make an informed decision.

Since investors ultimately hope to sell their shares at a substantial gain, or at least be able to liquidate their position at some future date, the next section, *Registration Rights*, becomes important. Investors will be given guaranteed registration rights after two years and piggyback rights in any future public offering.

The section entitled *Selection of Committee* describes the mechanics and approval process for any negotiations between the bank and the company.

Finally, the *Authorization* section emphasizes that the offering is being made by this memorandum only to selected investors. It directs investors to *The Williams Act* section and asks them to consult qualified legal counsel to determine if they are subject to the Act.

No. _____

PRIVATE PLACEMENT MEMORANDUM

NOT A PUBLIC OFFERING

ABC INDUSTRIES, INC.

$_____

Private Financing

(date)_____

(continued)

EXHIBIT 5-1 (*continued*)

PRIVATE PLACEMENT MEMORANDUM
NOT A PUBLIC OFFERING
ABC INDUSTRIES, INC. (ABC)
$_____
Private Financing

This memorandum contains certain information concerning ABC, which may not be generally known to the public as of the date hereof, and the offeree is cautioned that the Securities Act of 1933 and the Securities Exchange Act of 1934 and the rules and regulations of the Securities and Exchange Commission promulgated thereunder restrict the use and/or the dissemination of such information.

Neither this memorandum nor any of the information contained herein may be reproduced, used, or distributed in any other manner without the express written permission of ABC, and by accepting delivery of this memorandum any recipient hereof shall be required to, and hereby is deemed to, agree to return this numbered copy of the memorandum to ABC at _____(address)_____ if such recipient does not undertake to participate in the private financing contemplated hereby. Similarly, any such recipient shall be required to and hereby is deemed to agree not to reproduce, use, or distribute this memorandum, or to disseminate the contents hereof in violation of applicable state or federal laws or regulations.

THE OFFERING

It is proposed that ABC issue shares of its common stock without par value to a limited number of sophisticated investors who will purchase securities for investment only and not with a view toward their resale or distribution or for the account of others. The minimum purchase per investor will be $100,000 with the number of shares being subject to determination as hereinafter set forth (see "Conditions Precedent to Purchase"). The specific terms of purchase shall be set forth in a Purchase Agreement to be negotiated between ABC and a committee representing the subscribers hereto (see "Selection of Committee"). The shares of ABC are listed for trading on the __(name)__ Exchange.

LIMITATIONS OF OFFERING

The shares offered hereby are limited to certain institutional investors meeting the definition contained in Section 25102 (i) of the California Corporate Securities Law of 1968, as amended, and the regulations

---

EXHIBIT 5-1 (*continued*)

adopted thereunder, and to certain individual investors, who have a minimum net worth of $300,000 (excluding furniture and furnishings) and a minimum net income of $100,000, and who have experience in investments involving high risks (see "Risk Factors").

USE OF PROCEEDS

The $2,000,000 of proceeds shall be used by ABC as working capital and for other general corporate purposes.

CONDITIONS PRECEDENT TO PURCHASE

The purchase of the shares provided herein is subject to certain conditions relating to ABC's principal lender, _____ (name of bank)_____ ("bank"), as hereinafter enumerated. It is intended that a committee of three be selected by the subscribers (see "Selection of Committee") and that such committee will negotiate with management for ABC and officers of the bank to obtain the following conditions:

In the event that the aforesaid conditions are obtained, then the purchase price per share of the shares shall be equal to 85 percent of the book value. The book value shall be determined by the auditors selected by ABC for the purposes of examining its accounts for the current fiscal year.

In the event that a satisfactory arrangement is not achieved with the bank, or all of the shares offered herein are not purchasesd, then the escrow account shall be terminated and all monies deposited therein (see "Escrow") shall be returned to each subscriber herein and the purchase agreement will not be executed.

SUBSCRIPTION AGREEMENT AND ESCROW

Each offeree who desires to purchase shares offered hereby will do so by executing a Subscription Agreement, a copy of which is attached hereto, and by delivering a check covering the purchase price thereof to _____.

(*continued*)

EXHIBIT 5-1 (*continued*)

The proceeds will be deposited in an escrow account to be opened at
_____(name of bank)_____. If the conditions precedent to the execution of the purchase agreement are met, then said agreement will be signed by the committee and the monies held in escrow shall be transferred to ABC in exchange for the issuance to each investor of shares purchased thereby. All costs of escrow are to be borne by ABC.

RESTRICTED SECURITIES

The shares to be purchased by the partnership from ABC are not being registered under Section 5 of the Securities Act of 1933 as amended (the "Act"), in reliance by the issuer on the exemption provided under Section 4(2) of the Act or Rule 146 adopted by the Securities and Exchange Commission thereunder. The shares will bear a legend condition restricting transfer, and each investor will be required to execute an Investment Letter in a form satisfactory to counsel for ABC.

The shares will constitute "restricted securities" and as such can only be sold pursuant to registration under the Act or an exemption therefrom.

Although Rule 144 adopted by the Securities and Exchange Commission may be available for resales, it requires (1) a two-year holding period by the beneficial owner and (2) that ABC be current in its reporting requirements under Section 13(a) of the Securities Exchange Act of 1934, as amended.

ABC has agreed to provide registration rights under certain conditions to the investors (see "Registration Rights"), which will be contained in the purchase agreement.

RISK FACTORS

The purchase of shares as an investment is subject to the following substantial risks:

(List risks of investing in ABC)

EXHIBIT 5-1 (*continued*)

ACCESS TO FURTHER INFORMATION

ABC has agreed to provide any potential investor herein or a duly authorized offeree representative an opportunity to receive such additional information concerning its business operations as may be reasonably required, and in such connection, ABC will make available to such potential investors or their duly authorized offeree representative (during normal business hours and on reasonable notice) its responsible officers to answer questions.

REGISTRATION RIGHTS

ABC has agreed that it will negotiate with the committee (see "Selection of Committee") an undertaking by ABC to provide the investors with guaranteed registered rights at any time after two years from the purchase of its shares. In addition, ABC will provide "piggyback" registration rights under certain circumstances and conditions to be agreed upon. In general, it is the intent of ABC to provide the investor with the maximum liquidity while not disrupting its business operations or the trading markets.

SELECTION OF COMMITTEE

The subscribers hereto shall select a committee of three of its members who shall be authorized to negotiate with ABC and the bank (see "Conditions Precedent to Purchase" and "Registration Rights"). A list of subscribers shall be prepared by ABC, including those ineligible to serve on the committee, and it shall be transmitted to each subscriber who shall vote for three people to be on the committee. After negotiations have culminated with ABC and the bank, the committee shall present a report and a copy of the proposed Purchase Agreement at a meeting of the subscribers, which shall be noticed at least ten days prior thereto. A vote of two-thirds of the subscribers will be required to authorize the execution of the purchase agreement and each subscriber shall be bound by the vote thereby, provided, however, that in the event that the conversion of debt to equity by the bank does not result in eliminating the net deficit on the balance sheet of ABC, then any subscriber hereto may elect not to purchase shares. It is conceivable that certain officers and/or directors of ABC may become purchasers hereunder. Such purchasers shall not be eligible to be on the committee; however, such purchasers shall have equal voting rights with all other purchasers for the purpose of authorization herein. Upon receiving the

(continued)

EXHIBIT 5-1 (*continued*)

affirmative vote as provided above, the committee is authorized and directed pursuant to the Subscription Agreement to execute a purchase agreement containing substantially the same terms and conditions as provided in the form to be presented at said meeting.

AUTHORIZATION

No person has been authorized to give any information or to make any representations other than those contained in this memorandum in connection with the offer, and, if given or made, such other information or representations must not be relied upon as having been authorized by ABC. This memorandum does not constitute an offer or solicitation by anyone in any jurisdiction in which such offer or solicitation is not authorized or in which the person making such offer or solicitation is not authorized to do so, or to any person to whom it is unlawful to make such offer or solicitation.

This offering is made solely by the memorandum and attached documents, which is being distributed by certain officers and/or directors of ABC, who may become investors. No commissions are being paid to any such individual, and no agents, brokers, or dealers have been authorized to make an offering of the shares, and no person or entity is receiving a commission as a result of the sale of any shares offered hereby.

THE WILLIAMS ACT

It is possible that the group of purchasers herein will constitute a "person" under Section 13(d) of the Securities Exchange Act of 1934, or even if not, that any purchaser herein can be subject to the requirements of said section. It is suggested that all investors consult with their legal counsel to determine whether they are subject to said section and, if so, to ensure their compliance therewith.

If a company is privately owned, it may consider direct solicitation of investors. The investors may take a direct position in the company through either the purchase of existing shares or the issuance of new shares. The investors may form a separate partnership to execute the latter positions. The problem with this approach in the case of a private company is the difficulty encountered in attempting to provide the equity investor with the ability to liquidate his or her position at some future date. Since public markets are not available to the investor, the company may be forced into some buy-back formula that could severely affect future cash flow.

SELLING THE COMPANY

Sometimes the option of selling a troubled company can be viable. However, the business must fill certain needs of the potential buyer. Essential in selling a company is the skill to identify the primary intangible assets the selling company might offer the "would-be" buyer to offset the relatively unattractive financial statement.

Some of the more obvious advantages that the company can offer would-be sellers in the marketplace are as follows:

1. Specialized management capability
2. Excellent brand-name identification
3. A tax loss carry-forward that may be utilized
4. An existing product line that fits well with that of another company
5. A distribution network that can increase the buyer's customer base
6. Excellent profit potential if an increased cash flow were available
7. A special premium which is being offered the buyer
8. Certain assets that have great value to a buyer
9. Valuable patents or trademarks that have not been fully developed

Such lists will help the buyer prepare a corporate profile. Exhibit 5-2 is an example of a corporate profile. It is simplified to give you an opportunity to understand the essential content. In this case the company had an outside advising firm develop the profile. The *summary* section describes the various corporations and products, market position, and facilities; provides a general reference to the enclosed financial data; and gives some comments about the future and the company's position.

The *Company* section tells when key personnel, products, and entities were created or eliminated. This section would also describe any ownership interests in the business. The *Business* section describes in more detail the products manufactured, patents, type of equipment, space, and production capacity.

The *Marketing and Sales* section describes the company's customer profile and the organization and techniques for selling the various products. The *Employees* section gives a brief background of the key employees. The objective is to show a good balance of technical skill, executive competence, and long-term experience.

The *Officers and Directors* section identifies the key officers, their positions, and individual ownership interest. This section usually includes important résumé information about these top people. The *Financial* section, though brief in this exhibit, is normally many pages long. At a minimum it includes the comparative balance sheet and statement of earnings, all referenced to supporting notes. The *Facilities and Equipment* section describes the location and square footage breakdown of the various plants and offices. It normally includes a brief description of the flow of equipment used to produce the various products.

The *Competitors* section is quite important. It tells the reader where the company stands in relation to its competition and provides a good profile of the industry. The *Growth Prospects* section briefly describes the company's outlook. In more sophisticated and comprehensive presentations, pro forma financials are included along with supporting assumptions.

EXHIBIT 5-2
Corporate Profile of LMN Company

Table of Contents

(continued)

EXHIBIT 5-2
Corporate Profile of LMN Company (*continued*)

PRIVATE

Mr. John Doe, President
LMN Company
————— Street
—————, California, 99999

Dear Sir:

At your request, we have prepared a corporate profile of LMN Company and its subsidiaries. The purpose of this profile is to set forth sufficient data in a meaningful format which can be used to acquaint merger candidates with LMN.

The profile summarizes information we gathered through (1) discussions with Mr. John Doe, President of LMN, and other key company executives, and (2) a review of documents and other reports concerning the company which you supplied to us, and (3) a review of unaudited financial statements which have been prepared from the books, records, and other data without audit.

Since the nature of our engagement did not in any way contemplate the application of auditing procedures requisite to expressing an opinion on any financial data contained therein, we did not attempt to verify independently the information furnished to us.

We wish to express our appreciation for the cooperation received during the course of our engagement.

Yours truly,

(name of advisory company)

EXHIBIT 5-2
Corporate Profile of LMN Company (*continued*)

SUMMARY

LMN Company was organized in 19__ under the direction of Sam Jones. At that time the company was involved solely in the production and marketing of product A. In 19__ LMN-1 Company was formed in California with LMN given an exclusive contract for the sale of all production. After only a year of production, sales were so great that production was started in the location A area under LMN-2, a wholly owned subsidiary of LMN.

With competition growing and certain costs rising, LMN found it advantageous in 19__ to sell the product A business. In addition, the plant in location B was closed and the equipment moved to location A, thereby adding a complete line of product B to the LMN-2 line. Management believes that LMN Company and its wholly owned subsidiary, LMN-2 Inc., now have the largest selection of product B on the market. This line carries the well-known trade name "MN." LMN was dissolved in 19__ for simplification of operation, and the complete operation of manufacturing, selling, and shipping has been carried on by LMN-2.

There is ample floor space in the company's present plant to accommodate the installation of additional machinery to increase the present production of product B and/or to manufacture other articles in the opinion of management.

As indicated in the unaudited financial statement attached herein, sales decreased for the year ended December 31, 19__, by $_____. For the seven months ended [date], there was a decrease to $_____ down from $_____ for the comparable period in the prior year.

Company management has indicated that this decrease in sales and its corresponding decrease in profits are due to heavy competition and price cutting during the last 12 months, but management anticipates a sales turnaround and related improvement in profits in the future. This will depend, of course, on the ability to develop and successfully distribute new products.

LMN Company, with its large selection of product B and its experience in the development of new-size products, in the opinion of company management would appear to be in an excellent position to move into a significant number of new products using their expertise in the product B field.

THE COMPANY

History

The company was founded in 19__ by Sam Jones. The company produced and sold product A. Under Jones's guidance it grew, and in 19__

(continued)

EXHIBIT 5-2
Corporate Profile of LMN Company (*continued*)

the company was incorporated. Mr. Sam Smith joined the company at that time as vice president in charge of plant production.

Being introduced to the product B industry in 19___, and seeing the great potential it had, Mr. Jones and Mr. Smith looked for a source of production for this item. Through outside contact they were introduced to Ms. Pam Brown, a product B engineer, who had developed a special machine and at that time was looking for money to go into business.

With LMN Company putting up the money and Ms. Pam Brown's ideas and patents, they formed LMN-2 and located in location A. The company was formed for the sole purpose of manufacturing product B. Ms. Brown was president and manager of LMN-1 and Mr. Smith was vice president. LMN Company was given an exclusive contract for the sale of all production.

At that time LMN-1 was owned 50 percent by LMN and 50 percent by Ms. Pam Brown.

After a year or so, sales were so great that more production was needed in the area. LMN Company then started another wholly owned subsidiary, LMN-2, which manufactured product B in location A.

In 19___ Ms. Pam Brown sold her interest in LMN-1 and started her own business of manufacturing machinery. At present, Ms. Brown is still a source of supply for some molds and parts, which LMN Company and its subsidiary, LMN-2, buy.

With competition growing and certain costs rising, in 19___ LMN Company found it to its advantage to first sell the product A business to give the company more room in _____, and then to use this space by closing down the plant in _____, and moving the equipment to _____. This operation proved very successful as LMN was able to cut down on management, office help, and factory employees.

Shortly thereafter, Mr. Jones and Mr. Smith saw the great potential in product B to be used mainly for the purpose of carry-out food trade. They then added a complete line of molds to their existing line.

For added simplification of bookkeeping and operation, in 19___ LMN-1 was dissolved, and with the LMN Company operating as a holding company, the complete operation of manufacturing, selling, and shipping has been carried on by LMN-2.

BUSINESS

Production

At the present time the company produces and inventories 10 different sizes of product B-1 and 12 different sizes of product B-2. The plant

EXHIBIT 5-2
Corporate Profile of LMN Company (*continued*)

is so arranged that in a matter of only minutes molds of one size can be removed and another size put in its place, assuring excellent production capacity. The plant is also arranged so that one part of the plant can be operated independently of the rest without great expense. This has been accomplished by designing and constructing the plant in sections of complete units, having four boilers instead of only one, and utilizing a water-cooling system with several pumps instead of only one.

Because of the versatility of the machines, many different types of molds were purchased throughout the years. Therefore, if a certain size of product B is in great demand, molds of the necessary size may be changed on various machines, thereby greatly increasing production of the desired item.

Since changes and improvements must be made in all businesses, in 19__ Mr. Smith began to design and produce a new mold that would not only make better product B-1 and improve the production output but would at the same time cut down on operating costs.

In 19__ the company started rebuilding 26 of their machines and equipping them with the new molds. At the present time all but three of the machines are completed and the new molds are in place and operating. This switch to the new molds has been so successful that management believes they have almost paid for themselves in less than one year.

At present, the company has two types of machines in operation producing product B: 26 machines use 4 molds per machine and 7 machines take 10 molds per machine. Depending upon the type of molds being run, the total output of these machines on a five-day schedule is from X_1 to X_2 cases per day. The counting, stacking, and conveying are all done automatically, leaving only the placing of product B in the cartons and the sealing of the cartons to be done manually. By virtue of patents on certain specialized machines held by the company, the machines differ from any of its competitors.

Management believes that within the buildings occupied by the company, there is room to install additional machinery, either for producing additional product B or for manufacturing other product B–type articles which the company might wish to produce.

Marketing and Sales

The sales of the company are directed towards X distributors, Y supply companies, Z supply houses, and chain drug and grocery stores.

X houses and Y supply companies handle all sizes of product B, which makes them the best source of distribution for product B. Z supply houses deal mainly in X_3 sizes.

(continued)

EXHIBIT 5-2
Corporate Profile of LMN Company (*continued*)

The method of sales to these concerns by the company has been through brokers or manufacturer representatives. These people usually carry several other good lines of merchandise and thus can display all items at one time when they call on customers. The company pays a 5 percent commission to the brokers and manufacturer's representatives.

The company does not have salespeople of its own because of the higher cost involved. Experience has shown that it is not possible for a salesperson to handle only the one line of product B in a territory to make it profitable.

Employees

Mr. Sam Cohen has been plant foreman since 19___ and has complete charge of daily production, work layout, and shift changes. Along with his regular duties and knowledge of plant operations, he also does much of the major maintenance.

Mr. Sam O'Neil, an employee since 19___, is the boiler engineer as well as a pipefitter and mechanic and has full charge of all plant maintenance, steam, water, air, and electricity.

Ms. Pam Blanc has been with the company since 19___ and is lead person on the day shift, in charge of product B-1 production. Her main jobs are maintaining the machinery and supervising the operators and packers in her department.

Mr. Sam Polsky has been with the company since 19___, as a lead person and boiler engineer on the swing or graveyard shift. He rotates each month with Ms. Pam Green, who also has been with the company since 19___ as a boiler engineer. They are responsible for overseeing the complete operation of the plant and employees on their shift.

Mr. Sam Hanson has been with the company since 19___ and is in charge of all shipping and receiving. Mr. Hanson has been with the company longer than any other employee.

Ms. Pam Hayes started with the company in 19___ and is the full-charge bookkeeper.

Under these very capable and hard-working people are machine operators, inspectors, and packers, over 25 percent of whom have been with the company over seven years. The average number of employees varies between X_4 to X_5 depending on production demands.

The company gives all employees a medical plan and insurance after they have worked for the company more than 90 days. If family coverage is desired, the employee may obtain this insurance by paying an additional cost.

To try to hold down absenteeism which is very detrimental to production operation, the company has put two practices into effect. First,

---

EXHIBIT 5-2
Corporate Profile of LMN Company (*continued*)

vacation time is figured on a percentage of actual time worked the previous year, and second, for every 60 consecutive days worked without absence, an employee is given an extra day of pay at vacation time.

OFFICERS AND DIRECTORS

The officers and directors of the corporation are:

Name	Position	Stock Ownership (%)
Sam Smith	President	X_6
Pam Lowe	Vice President	X_7
James High	Secretary–treasurer	X_8
Mary Jones	Former officer	X_9
Total		100%

Sam Smith

Mr. Sam Smith has been vice president since 19__, in full charge of all production and the manufacturing of the product. He has engineered and directed the installation of all equipment as well as the development of new molds and machines, which have greatly reduced costs.

He has developed many of the conveyors, counters, and other machinery that has improved the process of making product A by making the operation more automatic.

Since the death of the company founder and president in January, Mr. Smith has been president of the company and has been in full charge of not only plant operations but sales policy and the complete operation of the company.

Mr. Smith is 49 years old.

Pam Lowe

Ms. Pam Lowe has been office manager since 19__. Her primary duties are the purchasing of all supplies and material. She supervises the routing of all orders for shipment, thereby building the company's reputation of selling service along with their product. Ms. Lowe was instrumental in developing the company's one-step invoicing and bill of lading procedure. After the death of the company founder and president in January, Ms. Lowe was appointed by the board of directors as vice president of the company.

Ms. Lowe is 48 years old.

(continued)

EXHIBIT 5-2
Corporate Profile of LMN Company (*continued*)

FINANCIAL

Following are the unaudited consolidated balance sheets of LMN Company and its subsidiaries as of December 31, 19__, and as of July 31, 19__, and 19__, and the related statements of operations and retained earnings (deficit) for the years ended December 31, 19__, and 19__, and for the seven months ended July 31, 19__, and 19__.

[Behind this should go the financial statements, supporting notes, and auditors' opinions related to the statements, which are not shown in this exhibit.]

FACILITIES AND EQUIPMENT

Location

The company is located in the northeast section of location A. This area is very advantageous to manufacturing for several reasons. The factory is located at the hub of three major highways which makes it ideal for shipping and receiving, for customers who wish to make will calls, and for employees traveling to and from work. The company is in a minority-group area, supplying a large labor force from which to choose employees.

Building

The building, although owned by another company and leased by LMN, was originally laid out and planned by Mr. Jones and Mr. Smith for the purpose of manufacturing product B-1. During its construction, several ideas for future expansion were kept in mind, such as a specially constructed roof to take additional water tower equipment and a large enough boiler room to take two additional boilers. An elevator was installed for basement warehousing, a sprinkler system for fire safety, and many other factors necessary for a good economical operation in the opinion of company management.

The building has a production area of approximately X_{10} square feet, office space area of approximately X_{11} square feet, and warehouse area of approximately X_{12} square feet.

The expanding room is self-contained for control of material, safety from fire, and cleanliness of operation.

The machines in the production area are laid out to give a constant

EXHIBIT 5-2

Corporate Profile of LMN Company (*continued*)

flow of material from expander to machines, then conveyed to inspectors and packers. The cartons are then sealed, palletized, and taken to the warehouse.

The printing department has an area all its own and contains two product B printing machines. This allows product B to be taken to the printing machines, printed, counted, stacked, and bagged; cartons to be sealed; and then everything to be delivered to the warehouse for shipping.

There is a full basement of approximately X_{13} square feet which contains two boiler rooms, a parking area, and some warehousing. The basement has a ramp to the street for cars and a freight elevator for the transferring of stock between floors.

Equipment

One of the boiler rooms contains three 35-horsepower boilers, water softeners, and makeup tanks to operate same. The second boiler room is much larger and contains one 150-horsepower boiler, water softeners, and makeup tanks. Management believes the equipment in this room is large enough to take care of two more 150-horsepower boilers, which could be added for future expansion.

There are four compressors in the basement with an addition on the outside of the building where two 75-horsepower compressors, making up the main source of air supply, are installed.

The warehouse has receiving and shipping docks as well as a rail spur by which raw material is received and rail shipments are made.

Each manufacturing area has its own entrance to the warehouse area for easy movement of materials.

COMPETITORS

[This section would list the major competitors by ranking, including the address, sales (if available) for the past five years, and relative share of the market held by each company.]

GROWTH PROSPECTS

Although the company management feels competition may continue in the product B field, they are of the same opinion that there are a significant number of items that could be made utilizing the same materials used for product B. The company would have to purchase new molds to make these items. In the broad sense, the company believes it could, with adequate financing, manufacture any item in the product B, C, or D line.

The potential tax aspects of a proposed transaction are extremely critical to its success. In general, corporate acquisitions are considered to be either taxable or tax-free for income tax purposes. While the tax status generally refers to the seller in the acquisition of property, the transaction is a major factor in determining the buyer's tax basis in the assets or stock acquired. A tax-free transaction generally occurs when the seller accepts stock in the acquiring company in exchange for the assets or the stock of the company being sold. This type of transaction is generally treated as a pooling of interests for tax purposes. In such a transaction, the financials of the two companies are aggregated. Tax on the transaction is deferred until the seller disposes of the stock. The seller's basis in the stock is, of course, the same as the tax basis in the stock being given up.

While one company may not acquire another merely to utilize the selling company's tax loss carry-forward, it may use that benefit for business purposes if other conditions are met. The ability of an acquiring company to use any part of this loss is a highly technical subject. Competent professional assistance should be sought in this matter. The Internal Revenue Code and the Consolidated Return Regulations restrict or limit the use of net operating carry-overs as well as other carry-overs where there is a substantial change of ownership in the stock of the corporation. This aspect of the code can often make it difficult to utilize the loss.

When a company understands what it has to offer a would-be buyer, has prepared a profile ready for delivery, and has studied the possible tax implications, it is ready to draw up a list of specific companies to contact. I suggest a worksheet listing the companies by probable order of interest, the known contact person in the company, the product line, the reason the potential company might be interested, and a proposed plan of action. If the company in crisis does not have sophisticated management or lacks any real personal contacts in the companies to be approached, it is best to seek professional assistance to get the job done.

MAKING INFORMAL CREDITOR ARRANGEMENTS

Your creditors are another source of funds. Depending on the extent of the crisis, a properly prepared presentation can convince your creditors that they should extend credit to higher levels or change payment terms. In certain cases, my clients have been able to convert a portion of their accounts payable to a long-term note. Often, sophisticated creditors, if they are convinced your plan will work, will become a source of funds. In certain situations, creditors also have accepted equity in return for debt reduction.

If the state of crisis is far along and the number of creditors involved is not excessive, an informal settlement may be possible. Keep in mind that a plan showing the settlement for each class of creditor must be developed. The creditors must also see the business plan so that they are convinced there is no better alternative than accepting the proposed loss. In my opinion, they must believe that they would lose even more if the company filed for bankruptcy. Informal composition requires the approval of *all* the creditors. It is, however, worth pursuing in many cases because these approvals can generally be used in a formal filing, should that become necessary. The effort is massive. Only a particular type of tenacious management can pull it off successfully. I generally suggest that the company generate a weekly status report like that shown in Table 5-2. In this plan, the company offered 40¢ on the dollar to all creditors with a balance under $500 and 10¢ on the dollar to all creditors owed more than $2,000. Creditors with a balance between $500 and $2,000 could take either 10 percent or $200, whichever was higher. We see on this report that of the 550 creditors over $500, representing $6,857,000, 391 had set-

TABLE 5-2
ABC Industries, Inc.
Settlement Status Report
As of _____
($000)

	Over $500				Under $500	Total
	Payables	Leases	Other	Total		
Settled						
Under $2,000 through	(231) $ 225		(2) $ 2			
Under $2,000	(1) 1				(491) $ 92	
Over $2,000 through	(140) 1,454	(8) $ 696	(9) 775	(391) $3,153	(1) / Lit (2) 1	(885) $3,246
Not settled						
Under $2,000 through	(49) 51		(3) 5		(56) 10	
Under $2,000 through	((1)) (1)				Lit (1)	
Over $2,000 through	(64) 1,725	(10) 1,178	(24) 696	(159) 3,704	((2))	(214) 3,714
Over $2,000 through						
Over $2,000 through	(10) · 50					
Accounts receivable credit balance (estimated)				(550) $6,857	(549) $103	(1099) $6,960
Percent settled				(71) $ 46	(90) $(90)	(81)

tled, representing $3,153,000. In other words, 71 percent of this class of creditors settled, representing 46 percent of the dollars in that class. Of the 549 creditors under $500, representing $103,000, 494 had settled, representing $93,000. In other words, 90 percent of this class of creditors settled, representing 90 percent of the dollars in that class. One of the biggest concerns in any creditor settlement program is making certain that the company can receive sufficient product to stay in business. While this option has its hazards, it should certainly be given serious consideration by any company in a crisis.

SEEKING OUTSIDE SOURCES OF LONG-TERM MONEY

At times a company can obtain funding outside the one source most businesses generally rely on: the bank. When the loan committee of the bank declines additional funding, the business executive often feels that there is no other place to turn. There are, of course, other institutions that can help. While the subject of locating outside financing sources is worthy of a separate book, this brief discussion will give the reader a general sense of direction.

Short-Term Sources. Business finance companies lend to a variety of companies, generally those of small and medium size. In general, they lend money against the security of assigned accounts receivable. They will also lend on a percentage of inventory and equipment. They are servicing that portion of the marketplace representing customers who could not qualify for bank credit. This source of funds understands that the borrowing relationship will continue for a number of years and will terminate as soon as the borrower's financial position has improved sufficiently to seek out lower-cost sources. The finance company will usually lend on a percentage of "eligible receivables," i.e., receivables that are 90 days old or less.

Another way that accounts receivable can be converted into

cash is through factoring. This is obtained primarily through factoring companies and some commercial banks. In typical accounts receivable financing arrangements, the borrower holds title to the accounts receivable while the lender expects the borrower to bear the losses if the accounts become uncollectible. The factoring company operates differently in that it purchases the accounts receivable from the company without recourse. Collection, therefore, becomes the factor's problem. Customers of the borrower are notified that the accounts have been sold and are asked to pay directly to the factor. This can cause great concern among vendors. If the process is not explained properly to the customers, they may interpret this as an act of liquidation. The factors, therefore, generally retain the right to screen and select those accounts receivable which are acceptable to them. All unaccepted accounts remain with the company and are handled at their own risk. The factors provide additional services. They handle most credit investigation, collect the receivables, and absorb the losses. The overall effective cost for this service is generally quite high.

Another avenue of short-term money that should not be overlooked is the private individual. You will usually be charged very high rates of interest and/or be required to provide a significant amount of equity. You may deal with a wealthy individual or you may negotiate with a syndication of many such people. I would be very cautious in dealing with private lenders and only look to this source when all others have been exhausted.

As suggested earlier in this chapter, you should not overlook the special credit that may be available from suppliers in problem situations. They have been known to convert outstanding overdue open accounts payables to a long-term note.

A fourth important source of funds that many companies fail to consider is the government agency. Sometimes government lending is offered when a given industry is suffering from severe economic problems created by external causes. This form of credit is also intended to fill the gaps left by other sources in the availability of credit. The creation of the Small Business Administration is an example of the latter. Special financial assistance is often available to suppliers of essential products, such as military items. States and other municipal jurisdictions have established development credit corporations to support employment and economic activity in their areas. They can be a valuable source of low-interest money if you qualify.

Long-Term Sources. New, long-term sources of money for a company in crisis are difficult to obtain. But since there may be a source of funds from time to time, I shall identify some of them. They include:

- Investment companies
- Retirement funds
- Pension funds
- Life insurance companies
- Fire and casualty insurance companies
- Individual investors

The Other Bank. Returning to the bank as a source of credit, I would like to suggest an approach for changing banks. After your company has bought time, used the time effectively, and developed the corporate strategy and business plan, you are ready to meet the other bank and review your problem with them. Show them your past track record in contrast to the current crisis. Explain to them how the current crisis came about, what you are doing to correct it, and when you expect the results to be reflected in the financial statements. Show them your business plan, and ask them at what point they would be willing to be a source of funds for your company. You may be pleasantly surprised at their willingness to work with you if your case is well presented. You may ask, "Why won't my existing bank work with me if we can survive the crisis?" This is a rational question that I'm afraid has no rational answer. Banks have long memories. Once you have gotten into trouble with them, it is often time to move out. Think of it as a large revolving door. You exit bank A and move on to bank B, while a company no better than you moves to bank A after exiting bank B. I have asked bankers why this happens and must admit that I can't understand their reasons either!

REPLACING MANAGEMENT

In order to get your debt restructured, to obtain a private placement, to get outside funds, or to obtain the cooperation of your creditors, you may face the most painful decision of all: some of the top management people may have to go. Lenders must be careful about interfering with management and may suggest the changes in the existing organization and personnel in some oblique fashion. Banks, with their long memories, will sometimes require a management change before giving significant monetary assistance. Creditors will be more verbal. In come cases they will demand a personnel change as the price of going along with an informal composition.

A fundamental credibility crisis must be faced. Lenders ask, "How can the same people who got us into trouble now show us a plan for getting out of trouble? If they knew how to avoid it in the first place, they would have never gotten into trouble." This kind of circular logic can prove deadly.

Replacing key executives is a delicate issue. Often some top management can stay, but it seems in these cases that some blood must be spilled. So do not be surprised when you hear the mob outside clamoring for your head on a plate, even if the cause of the crisis was totally beyond your control. "Goats" are needed, and they will be found!

Be assured that with artful negotiations, the bulk of management can in general be saved. It is, in fact, imperative that the key personnel be saved.

Chapter 6

Alarm-Reporting System

Most executives have been trained to manage the profit and loss statements. They are usually familiar with such concepts as profit center reporting, responsibility center reporting, flexible and static budgets, and standard cost control. In the back of their Management Reporting Package, there was most likely some limited balance sheet and funds flow data that went virtually ignored. After all, "If the earnings are there, if the predicted earnings per share are achieved, we are in good shape, right?" *Wrong!* That balance sheet that you always wanted to know about but were afraid to ask will now become your "bible." You will learn to study every element so that funds can be made available when needed to keep the company alive. In many cases, the profit and loss statement will become useless. In fact, it will sometimes be necessary to sacrifice profits in order to maximize the short-term use of funds. Executives, faced with this new set of decision-making rules, will often panic, because they are traveling on uncharted waters, operating in an environment for which they have little experience and training.

Top management will need an alarm-reporting system to get through the crisis. A day in a troubled organization is like a month in a healthy company. Not only must decisions be made more rapidly but prompt reporting must be provided to ensure the executive that each decision is producing the desired result.

The exact format of the reporting system will vary with each company, but there are some basics that apply to most situations. This chapter will explain these basics and provide examples.

BASIC INFORMATION

Some of the basic information should include:

1. A weekly cash plan and daily cash control against plan
2. Worksheets for the weekly cash meeting, including:
   a. Weekly recommendations
   b. Weekly projects
3. A monthly planning package

All the above is utilized in addition to the overall corporate plans, which provide monthly balance sheet, profit and loss, and cash-flow information.

WEEKLY AND DAILY CASH PLANNING

The focal point in a crisis environment is the weekly cash meeting. It should be run by the chief operating officer and include all executives who are responsible for cash receipts and disbursements. These executives should come to the meeting prepared. For example, if they are responsible for disbursements, they should know the priorities of the cash requirements in their department so that they can operate effectively in a particular week in accordance with the adequacy of the cash flow. If they are responsible for receipts, they should separate expected cash inflow by level of probability. Planning of disbursements should not be based on any "blue sky" assumptions about receipts. No excuse for absence should be acceptable; *everyone invited must attend and be prepared.* Such meetings should be held on Monday morning to ensure that all key personnel are pointed in the right direction. The meeting should begin with a review of the previous week's actual performance in comparison to the plan. The status of projects undertaken in previous meetings should be reviewed by the responsible executives. The controller should prepare a preliminary cash plan based on meetings held with key people separately on Friday.

The weekly cash plan, Table 6-1, should be reviewed to see if any major disbursements are projected on the horizon. For example, if we are having our weekly meeting on May 3, it is important to recognize that on May 24, $112,000 must be made available for sales tax. It may, therefore, be necessary to build a surplus over the next few weeks.

Next, we look at what happened the previous week. In Table 6-2, we anticipated receipts of $1,020,000 and disbursements of $820,000, generating a positive weekly cash flow of $200,000. Instead, we collected $896,000 and disbursed $848,000, generating a cash flow of only $48,000.

A review of the receipts actually shows that wholesale sales exceeded the plan by $99,000, while retail sales fell short by $235,000. We would ask the executive responsible for retail operations to give us a store-by-store analysis. "Why," we might ask, "weren't disbursements cut back during the week when it became clear that receipts would fall short?" Little can be done with payroll. It appears that disbursements were cut back to the notes and realty, location A vendors, and advertisers. Yet corporate disbursements were $55,000 over plan, and $24,000 in sales tax was paid when none was planned. These deviations must be analyzed and their impact on future periods understood.

The chief financial officer then presents a sheet similar to Table 6-2, with only the planning column completed, for the coming week. The responsible executives review their detail schedules and either accept their part of the plan or negotiate for modifications.

TABLE 6-1
ABC Industries, Inc.
Cash Plan
($000)

	4/5	4/12	4/19	4/26	5/3	5/10	5/17	5/24	5/31	6/7	6/14
Receipts											
Real estate	—	—	800[2]	230[1] 250[3]	300[4]	—	240[5]	—	—	—	—
Wholesale sales	250	250	300	300	300	300	300	300	300	250	250
Other	50	75	100	100	100	100	100	100	100	100	—
Retail—1	530	540	550	560	570	580	590	600	610	610	610
Retail—2	50	75	160	160	160	160	160	160	160	160	160
Total	880	940	1,910	1,600	1,430	1,140	1,390	1,160	1,170	1,120	1,020
Disbursements											
Location A	70	70	70	70	70	70	70	70	70	70	70
Payroll	42	42	42	42	42	42	42	42	42	42	42
Location B	32	32	26	17	17	16	15	15	15	13	13
Payroll	36	29	23	16	12	8	7	6	5	3	2
Corporate	20	20	20	20	20	20	15	15	15	15	15
Payroll	45	18	35	14	27	12	27	12	27	12	27
National vendors	110	90	90	90	90	90	90	75	75	75	75
Transfers	220	229	269	271	273	275	278	280	282	262	262
Notes and realty	29	70	18	39	24	25	35	28	23	4	29
Insurance (liability)	—	35	—	—	42	—	—	—	—	47	—
Total	604	635	593	579	617	558	579	543	554	543	535

	1	2	3	4	5	6	7	8	9	10	11
Retail	54	37	54	37	54	37	54	37	54	37	54
Payroll	1	1	1	1	1	1	1	1	1	1	1
Insurance	10	10	12	12	12	12	12	12	12	12	12
Utilities and rent	18	18	20	20	20	20	20	20	20	20	20
Advertising											
Payables trade and	50	50	50	60	70	70	70	70	70	70	70
sublet	50	10	75	—	—	18	—	112	—	—	—
Sales tax and DMV	—	—	—	15	10	13	10	15	20	18	10
Interest	3	5	5	10	10	7	5	5	10	7	10
Curtailments and notes	7	2	3	3	3	3	3	3	3	3	3
Refunds	2	—	—	—	—	—	—	—	—	—	—
Payoffs—trade-in	40	40	60	60	60	60	60	60	60	60	60
Payoffs—Repo	20	20	20	20	20	20	10	10	10	10	20
Payoffs—Flr.	65	65	65	65	65	65	65	65	65	65	65
	270	258	365	303	325	326	310	410	325	303	325
Total Disbursements	874	893	958	882	942	884	889	953	879	846	860
Cash Flow	6	47	952	718	488	256	501	207	291	274	160

¹CP sale.
²Beginning of EFC flooring on week ending 4/19.
³AS sale.
⁴RB sale.
⁵Foreign funds week ending 5/17.

113

TABLE 6-1 (*Continued*)
ABC Industries, Inc.
Cash Plan
(*$000*)

	6/21	6/28	7/5	7/12	7/19	7/26	8/2	8/9	8/16	Total
Receipts										
Real estate	—	—	—	—	—	—	—	—	—	1,820
Wholesale sales	250	250	200	200	200	200	200	200	200	5,000
Other	—	—	—	—	—	—	—	—	—	925
Retail—1	610	610	610	590	570	550	530	510	490	11,420
Retail—2	160	160	160	160	160	160	160	160	160	3,005
Total	1,020	1,020	970	950	930	910	890	870	850	22,170
Disbursements										
Location A										
Payroll	70	70	70	70	70	70	70	70	70	1,400
Location B	42	42	42	42	42	42	42	42	42	840
Payroll	12	10	10	10	10	10	10	10	10	303
Corporate	2	2	2	2	2	2	2	2	2	165
Payroll	15	15	15	15	15	15	15	15	15	330
National vendors	12	27	12	27	12	27	12	27	12	424
Transfers	75	75	75	75	75	75	75	75	75	1,625
Notes and realty	262	262	242	238	233	229	225	221	217	5,030
Insurance (liability)	16	7	18	18	18	18	18	18	18	473
	—	—	35	—	—	—	35	—	—	194
	506	510	521	497	477	488	504	480	461	10,784

Retail										
Payroll	37	54	37	54	37	54	37	54	37	910
Insurance	1	1	1	1	1	1	1	1	1	20
Utilities and rent	12	12	12	12	12	12	12	12	12	236
Advertising	20	20	20	20	20	20	20	20	20	396
Payables trade and sublet	70	70	70	70	70	70	70	70	70	1,330
Sales tax and DMV	18	—	112	—	18	—	112	28	28	531
Interest	13	10	15	20	13	10	15	15	15	240
Curtailments and notes	7	5	5	10	7	5	5	5	5	135
Refunds	3	3	3	3	3	3	3	3	3	58
Payoffs—trade-in	60	60	60	60	60	60	60	60	60	1,160
Payoffs—Repo	20	10	10	10	10	10	10	10	10	280
Payoffs—Flr.	65	65	65	65	65	65	65	65	65	1,300
	326	310	410	325	316	310	410	343	326	6,596
Total Disbursements	832	820	931	822	793	798	914	823	787	17,380
Cash Flow	188	200	39	128	137	112	(24)	47	63	4,790

115

TABLE 6-2
ABC Industries, Inc.
Daily Cash Control
($000)

	Responsible Executive	Plan	Week Ended 6/28					
			6/23	6/24	6/25	6/26	6/27	Total
Receipts								
Real estate	A							
Wholesale sales	B	250	151	67	62	66	3	349
Other	C							
Retail—1	D	610	148	93	102	100	92	535
Retail—2	E	160						
Other		—	2	—	—	10	—	12
Total		1,020	301	160	164	176	95	896
Disbursements								
Location A	F	70	8	5	20	3	3	39
Payroll	F	42	—	—	—	—	33	33
Location B	G	12	2	11	4	4	2	23
Payroll	G	2	—	—	—	1	4	5
Corporate	H	15	6	21	7	15	13	62
Payroll	H	27	2	1	2	—	30	35
National vendors	I	75	9	24	47	—	—	80
Transfers	I	262	51	31	87	43	—	212
Notes and realty	J	7	—	—	27	6	—	33
Insurance (liability)	J							
		510	78	93	194	72	85	522

Retail

								Total
Payroll	K	54	1	8	4	—	25	38
Insurance	K	1	—	1	1	7	—	2
Utilities and rent	K	12	5	5	1	2	—	18
Advertising	K	20	—	4	1	14	1	8
Payables	K	70	10	24	14	2	18	80
Sales tax and DMV	A	—	13	5	—	—	4	24
Interest	A	10	—	—	1	—	—	—
Curtailments and notes	A	5	1	1	1	1	—	3
Refunds	A	3	1	1	1	—	1	4
Payoffs—trade-in	A	60	21	42	9	25	13	110
Payoffs—Repo		10	—	—	—	—	—	—
Payoffs—Flr.		65	10	9	—	—	—	9
Other—special		—	—	13	—	7	—	30
Flr.		310	62	112	32	58	62	326
Total Disbursements		820	140	205	226	130	147	848
Cash Flow from Operations		200	161	(45)	(62)	46	(52)	48

This weekly cycle of planning the coming week's cash flow after reviewing the performance of the previous week is essential to good cash management. All executives whose daily decisions affect cash must be involved in this weekly process. The weekly cash plan should be available 15 to 20 weeks into the future. It should be updated weekly on a sliding basis. Particular emphasis should be given to the source, timing, and amounts of major receipts and disbursements, as shown in Table 6-1. The plan and the report, if at all possible, should fit on $8\frac{1}{2} \times 11$ inch sheets. The creation of too many classifications will make the task of gathering information and making decisions cumbersome.

The idea is to have a brief, organized meeting at the start of the week and then let everyone leave with a clear set of marching orders. It is important that certain rules be observed in the management of cash in a crisis.

1. Centralize responsibility under one person.
2. Centralize check signing wherever possible.
3. In a multilocation operation, each location should accumulate the checks to be paid each day, then contact the corporate office for approval. Checks that are not critical should be paid out of the corporate office.
4. The sum of all checks paid cannot exceed the daily receipts of the previous day. Top-level approval is required to violate this rule.
5. A procedure should be arranged with the company's bank to deal with disbursements that must be made in excess of receipts. This can be accomplished through some form of short-term loan arrangement. Under any conditions, never surprise the bank.
6. Disbursements should be made as late as possible without hampering the company's ability to run its business. When the cash-flow problem is severe, it is rarely worthwhile to take the discount and pay early.

7. All bank accounts must be authorized by the chief executive officer. All checks in excess of $X should require at least two signatures. If at all possible, big-dollar checks should be signed by corporate.
8. The basic internal controls related to cash receipts and disbursements should be followed precisely. This includes control over mail receipts. over-the-counter currency, delinquent accounts, evidence required for payment of checks, and storage of unused checks. The underlying concept of internal control is to segregate work responsibility so that no one person can use the funds of the company improperly without collusion.

I emphasize these rules because the top executive must take personal responsibility in this area. Often, when the top executive is a marketing, sales, production, or engineering type, the executive will tell me, "I don't know anything about finance. That's the job of my financial officer." My answer is simple: "Start learning now!!" The buck stops here with the top executive! The chief executive must know where literally each dollar is coming from and how it is going to be spent. Check signing should be in the hands of as few people as possible. The bank must be in the role of a working partner and must, therefore, be kept fully informed.

At this stage, good internal controls become more important than ever. When a company is in turmoil, it becomes a tempting target for those people who might want to misappropriate cash for their own benefit.

WORKSHEETS

The format of the worksheets will vary by company. Shown in Exhibit 6-1 is a package used by one company which we shall refer to as the ABC Corporation. In addition to keeping the weekly cash information discussed above, this company maintains an updated version of its annual balance sheet, income statement, and cash-flow business plan by month. The company feels this overview is helpful both in dealing with day-to-day problems and in assisting management in separating the "forest from the trees." These forecasts are illustrated in Schedules 6-1 to 6-3 of Exhibit 6-1. Schedule 6-4 is the worksheet that lists the projects agreed to in the previous week to ensure that they are being carried out by the responsible executive in a timely manner. Schedule 6-5 presents the weekly flow in the near term, while Scheule 6-6 measures last week's actual performance against the plan as well as performance for the year to date. Since this company utilizes accounts receivable financing, it is also necessary in Schedule 6-6 to show the availability of funds for borrowing. In Schedule 6-7 the controller, after meetings with the appropriate executives, develops a conservative, optimistic, and expected cash-flow forecast. The conservative forecast only counts receipts that are highly reliable, assuming that all anticipated disbursements must be paid. The optimistic schedule assumes that all anticipated collections are received and that disbursements are delayed wherever possible. The "expected" column is simply the financial officer's judgments, based on past experience, of what will in all actuality occur the following week. All payments to vendors are supported by a detailed schedule showing the name of the vendor, aged amount owed, terms, and amount to be paid. Schedule 6-8 shows the aged accounts receivable. This schedule is used to initiate action to collect on problem accounts before they become seriously delinquent.

Schedule 6-9 shows the aged accounts payable. This schedule is used to make certain that the company is paying its key vendors properly and that funds are not disbursed unnecessarily to vendors who are not essential to the survival of the business.

Schedule 6-10 projects inventory balances, purchases, and commitments over future weeks. This schedule helps to ensure that slow-moving inventory is being moved out and that the company is not overcommitting funds for the purchase of new inventory.

At the conclusion of the meeting, recommendations are made to correct problems related to assets, liabilities, revenues, expenses, etc., as shown in Schedule 6-11. The accepted recommendations are then converted into projects and assigned responsibilities and due dates, as shown in Schedule 6-12. Note that Schedule 6-12 of week 1 becomes Schedule 6-4 of week 2.

The great value of these worksheets is that they force an orderly management of the company throughout the crisis. By requiring responsible executives to do the planning necessary to keep the meetings short, this method allows for prompt and informed decision making.

EXHIBIT 6-1
ABC Corporation
Weekly Cash Management Package

(continued)

EXHIBIT 6-1

ABC Corporation Weekly Cash Management Package

SCHEDULE 6-1

ABC Corporation

Business Projection for the Fiscal Year Ending _____

Balance Sheet

	June–Aug.	Sept.	Oct.	Nov.	Dec.	Jan.	Feb.	March	April	May
Cash	$ (1,500)	$ (500)	$ 4,500	$ 5,000	$ 5,000	$ 5,000	$ 5,000	$ 5,000	$ 5,000	$ 5,000
Accounts receivable	871,800	887,000	904,200	917,200	927,800	937,000	946,100	955,200	963,200	970,400
Inventory	702,700	710,300	719,100	725,000	729,200	732,400	735,300	738,100	740,700	743,300
Other	270,900	252,000	247,000	228,700	210,400	167,100	148,800	130,500	112,200	93,900
Total noncash	1,845,400	1,849,300	1,870,300	1,870,900	1,867,400	1,836,500	1,830,200	1,823,800	1,816,100	1,807,600
Total current	1,843,900	1,848,800	1,874,800	1,875,900	1,872,400	1,841,500	1,835,200	1,828,800	1,821,100	1,812,600
Property, plant, and equipment	600,200	600,200	600,200	600,200	506,000	506,000	506,000	506,000	506,000	506,000
Allowance for depreciation	262,800	267,800	272,800	277,800	207,600	215,700	223,800	231,900	240,000	248,100
Net fixed assets	337,400	332,400	327,400	322,400	298,400	290,300	282,200	274,100	266,000	257,900
Other assets	2,200	2,200	2,200	2,200	2,200	2,200	2,200	2,200	2,200	2,200
Total assets	$2,183,500	$2,183,400	$2,204,400	$2,200,500	$2,173,000	$2,134,000	$2,119,600	$2,105,100	$2,089,300	$2,072,700

Current liabilities									
Accounts payable—trade	$ 865,000	$ 877,200	$ 838,800	$ 899,600	$ 909,400	$ 907,500	$ 898,200	$ 899,300	$ 879,100	$ 873,000
Receivable and inventory loans payable	566,100	603,400	638,800	671,900	698,600	753,800	775,100	781,700	781,700	781,700
Current portion of long-term debt	90,000	90,000	90,000	90,000	90,000	90,000	100,000	100,000	100,000	103,600
Income taxes payable	86,900	71,400	56,500	42,300	30,900	22,400	14,500	9,600	5,900	5,700
Total current liabilities	1,608,000	1,642,000	1,674,100	1,703,800	1,728,900	1,773,700	1,787,800	1,790,600	1,766,700	1,764,000
Contracts payable									
Notes payable	155,200	163,200	171,200	179,200	187,200	195,200	221,400	230,500	239,500	242,700
Stockholder loans payable	159,400	159,400	159,400	159,400	159,400	159,400	159,400	159,400	159,400	159,400
Total long-term debt	314,600	322,600	330,600	338,600	346,600	354,600	380,800	389,900	398,900	402,100
Total liabilities	1,922,600	1,964,600	2,004,700	2,042,400	2,075,500	2,128,300	2,168,600	2,180,500	2,165,600	2,166,100
Capital stock	37,100	37,100	37,100	37,100	37,100	37,100	37,100	37,100	37,100	37,100
Retained earnings	113,000	87,600	63,300	40,100	21,400	7,600	(5,200)	(13,200)	(19,300)	(19,700)
Total stockholders' equity	150,100	124,700	100,400	77,200	58,500	44,700	31,900	23,900	17,800	17,400
Total liabilities and stockholders' equity	$2,072,700	$2,089,300	$2,105,100	$2,119,600	$2,134,000	$2,173,000	$2,200,500	$2,204,400	$2,183,400	$2,183,500

(continued)

EXHIBIT 6-1

ABC Corporation Weekly Cash Management Package (*continued*)

SCHEDULE 6-2
ABC Corporation
Business Projection for the Fiscal Year Ending _____
Income Statement

	June–Aug.	Sept.	Oct.	Nov.	Dec.	Jan.	Feb.	March	April	May	Total
Sales (net)	$1,447,200	$484,700	$529,900	$534,800	$539,500	$545,300	$555,100	$564,700	$568,100	$571,400	$6,340,700
Cost of sales	819,200	269,900	289,200	289,200	289,200	289,200	290,800	292,500	294,100	295,800	3,419,100
Gross profit	628,000	214,800	240,700	245,600	250,300	256,100	264,300	272,200	274,000	275,600	2,921,600
Selling expenses	380,000	134,300	149,700	150,200	149,600	150,300	151,500	152,600	153,100	153,500	1,724,800
General and administrative	192,200	65,200	66,700	68,100	69,900	69,900	69,900	69,900	69,900	69,900	811,600
Other income	700	—	—	—	3,700	—	—	—	—	—	4,400
Profit (loss) before interest	56,500	15,300	24,300	27,300	34,500	35,900	42,900	49,700	51,000	52,200	389,600
Interest	41,500	14,700	14,500	14,400	13,800	13,600	12,800	12,300	11,800	11,300	160,700
Profit (loss) before taxes	15,000	600	9,800	12,900	20,700	22,300	30,100	37,400	39,200	40,900	228,900
Provision for income taxes	5,700	200	3,700	4,900	7,900	8,500	11,400	14,200	14,900	15,500	86,900
Net income	$ 9,300	$ 400	$ 6,100	$ 8,000	$ 12,800	$ 13,800	$ 18,700	$ 23,200	$ 24,300	$ 25,400	$ 142,000

ABC Corporation
Business Projection for the Fiscal Year Ending _____
Cash-Flow Statement

	Sept.	Oct.	Nov.	Dec.	Jan.	Feb.	March	April	May
Cash at start	$(1,500)	$ (500)	$ 4,500	$ 5,000	$ 5,000	$ 5,000	$ 5,000	$ 5,000	$ 5,000
Add:									
Net income	400	6,100	8,000	12,800	13,800	18,700	23,200	24,300	25,400
Decrease current assets	—	—	—	3,500	30,900	6,300	6,400	7,700	8,500
Increase current liabilities	2,700	23,900	—	—					
Depreciation	5,000	5,000	5,000	8,100	8,100	8,100	8,100	8,100	8,100
Long-term borrowing	—	—	—	55,000					
Sale of fixed assets	—	—	—	80,900					
Total provided	8,100	35,000	13,000	160,300	52,800	33,100	37,700	40,100	42,000
Less:									
Increase current assets	3,900	21,000	600	14,100	44,800	25,100	29,700	32,100	34,000
Decrease current liabilities	—	—	2,800	—					
Pay down long-term debt	3,200	9,000	9,100	81,200	8,000	8,000	8,000	8,000	8,000
Purchase of fixed assets	—	—	—	65,000					
Total used	7,100	30,000	12,500	160,300	52,800	33,100	37,700	40,100	42,000
Total provided (used) for period	1,000	5,000	500	-0-	-0-				
Ending cash balance	$ (500)	$ 4,500	$ 5,000	$ 5,000	$ 5,000	$ 5,000	$ 5,000	$ 5,000	$ 5,000

(continued)

EXHIBIT 6-1
ABC Corporation
Weekly Cash Management Package (*continued*)

SCHEDULE 6-4
ABC Corporation
Projects to Be Accomplished for Week Beginning _____

Project	Responsibility	Result

EXHIBIT 6-1

ABC Corporation Weekly Cash Management Package (*continued*)

SCHEDULE 6-5
ABC Corporation
Weekly Cash-Flow Forecast

	Week	Week	Week	Week	Week	Week	Week	Week	Week	Week
Collections										
Account payable—old										
Account payable—new										
Freight										
UPS										
Payroll										
Rent—building										
Rent—IBM										
Rent—automobiles										
Contracts—fork lift, etc.										
Note										
Printing machine note										
Accounts receivable—inv. interest										
Term note										
Aircraft (net of income)										
Total disbursements										
Net weekly increase (decrease)										

(continued)

127

EXHIBIT 6-1
ABC Corporation Weekly Cash Management Package (*continued*)

SCHEDULE 6-6
ABC Corporation
Cash-Flow Historical Summary
Week Ended _____

	Previous Week			Year to Date	
	Budget	Actual		Budget	Actual
Collections					
Accounts payable—old					
Accounts payable—new					
Freight					
Payroll					
Rent—building					
Rent—IBM					
Rent—automobiles					
Contracts—fork lift, etc.					
Note					
Printing machine note					
Accounts receivable—inv. interest					
Term note					
Aircraft (net of income)					
Total disbursements					
Net increase (decrease)					
Balance due bank	Previous week			Current week	
Availability					

EXHIBIT 6-1
ABC Corporation
Weekly Cash Management Package (*continued*)

SCHEDULE 6-7
ABC Corporation
Cash Flow
Current Week

	Conservative	Expected	Optimistic
Collections[1]	————	————	————
Accounts payable—old[2]	————	————	————
Accounts payable—new	————	————	————
Freight	————	————	————
Payroll	————	————	————
Rent—building	————	————	————
Rent—IBM	————	————	————
Rent—automobiles	————	————	————
Contracts—fork lift, etc	————	————	————
Note	————	————	————
Printing machine note	————	————	————
Accounts receivable— inv. interest	————	————	————
Term note	————	————	————
Total disbursements	————	————	————
Net weekly increase (decrease)	————	————	————
Recommended bank pay down	————	————	————

[1]Calculated based on projected revenue.
[2]Controller has detailed schedule to support noting specific vendors.

(continued)

EXHIBIT 6-1
ABC Corporation
Weekly Cash Management Package (*continued*)

SCHEDULE 6-8
ABC Corporation
Accounts Receivable

	0–30	31–60	61–90	Over 90	Total
Accounts receivable beginning of month[1,2]	____	____	____	____	____
Sales—week 1	____	____	____	____	____
Collections—week 1	____	____	____	____	____
Accounts receivable week 1[2]	____	____	____	____	____
Sales—week 2	____	____	____	____	____
Collections—week 2	____	____	____	____	____
Accounts receivable week 2	____	____	____	____	____
.					
.					
.					
Accounts receivable week 4[1]	____	____	____	____	____
(Projected receivables)	____	____	____	____	____
Difference	____	____	____	____	____
Accounts receivable week 8[1]	____	____	____	____	____

[1]Monthly balances reconciled to control account.
[2]Number of days sales in accounts receivable calculated on a weekly basis.

EXHIBIT 6-1

ABC Corporation Weekly Cash Management Package (*continued*)

SCHEDULE 6-9
ABC Corporation
Accounts Payable and Accrued Liabilities

	Old					New		
	0–30	31–60	61–90	Over 90	Total	Inv.	Other	Total
Balance—beginning of month[1]								
New payables								
Payments								
Balance week 1								
.								
.								
Balance week 8								
(Projected payables)[2]								
Difference								

[1]Beginning balances generated from aged trial balance which has been reconciled to the control account.
[2]Difference between projection generated monthly.

(continued)

EXHIBIT 6-1
ABC Corporation
Weekly Cash Management Package (*continued*)

SCHEDULE 6-10
ABC Corporation
Inventory and Purchases

	Projected	Actual	Inventory Balance			
			Class A	Class B	Class C	Other
Week 1	————	————	————	————	————	————
.						
.						
.						
Week 4	————	————	————	————	————	————
(Projected						
inventory)	————	————	————	————	————	————
Difference	————	————	————	————	————	————

EXHIBIT 6-1
ABC Corporation
Weekly Cash Management Package (*continued*)

SCHEDULE 6-11
ABC Corporation
Weekly Recommendations

Assets

Liabilities

Revenues

Expenses

Other

(continued)

EXHIBIT 6-1
ABC Corporation
Weekly Cash Management Package (*continued*)

SCHEDULE 6-12
ABC Corporation
Projects to Be Accomplished for Week Beginning _____

Project	Responsibility	Result

MONTHLY PLANNING PACKAGE

In addition to the monthly balance sheet, profit and loss, and cash-flow statements, which generally show comparisons against budgets and prior year, a graphical presentation of the more important accounts is often useful.

Shown in Exhibit 6-2 is the monthly package used by the XYZ Corporation.

Schedule 6-1 summarizes cash balances and bank debt in graph form. Schedule 6-2 summarizes aged accounts receivables along with a supporting graph showing days outstanding. This schedule also depicts monthly activity related to property plant and equipment. Schedule 6-3 outlines and demonstrates in graph form the inventory by classification against time. It also shows the backlog position and provides an employee count against forecast.

Schedule 6-4 shows the magnitude of accounts payable by month and reveals the aging of these accounts. Schedule 6-5 summarizes earnings against forecast; Schedule 6-6 summarizes sales against forecast. Schedule 6-7 divides the revenue and expenses on the monthly profit and loss statements into greater detail so that management can better control sources of revenue and costs against the forecast.

Let us examine these graphs and reports in Exhibit 6-2 to see how they are used. The cash chart shows that our actual cash balance is almost $20,000 in excess of the forecast. This is a good sign unless the increased cash position was created by additional borrowing. The chart on bank debt reveals that while actual debt increased over the previous month, it is substantially below the forecasted level. Analysis of trade accounts receivable in Schedule 6-2 shows an excellent collection effort. The days outstanding has been reduced from a peak of 52.7 days to 23.1 days. The analysis of property, plant, and equipment shows us at a glance that little activity occurred in these accounts during the month. In Schedule 6-3 we can observe a slight increase in inventory with no dramatic change in the relationship between work in process and material and stores. The backlog analysis, however, gives us cause for concern. Only $4,828 in orders were received, reducing the backlog by $190,885 (from $758,981 in the prior month to $568,096 in the current month). The overall employee count is over forecast, but when we analyze the salary dollars later, we will see the actual mix is composed of less expensive personnel. Schedule 6-4 shows that the XYZ Corporation is able to maintain its aging at 60 days or less. The jump in the balance during the previous month was a result of a major special purchase. Schedule 6-5 clearly demonstrates that the company is exceeding its year-to-date earnings forecast by $38,000. Earnings are, however, forecast to drop precipitously later in the year, and management should be taking action to guard against this forecast loss. The earnings performance is even more impressive when we examine Schedule 6-6, which shows that actual sales is running somewhat below the forecast.

Schedule 6-7 shows in schedule form all major profit and loss accounts against plan for the month and year to date. We can immediately see that the year-to-date sales fall short by $208,983, primarily because of the H/O division. This sales difference is not fully reflected in lost profits because expenses were reduced by $247,494 in comparison to budget, creating a net profit impact of $38,511.

Yet certain accounts may need further analysis. At a reduced sales level, why is operating supplies $10,000 over forecast on a year-to-date basis? We would have expected telephone, travel, and freight expenses to decline, yet they have remained constant. Careful analysis and appropriate action related to these matters could further improve the profits of XYZ Corporation even though sales are below forecast.

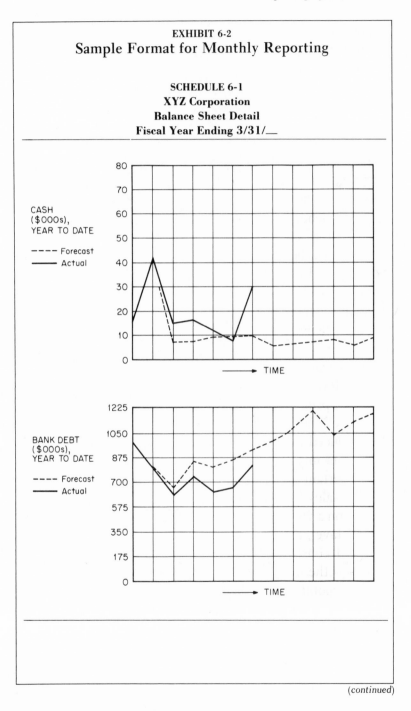

EXHIBIT 6-2
Sample Format for Monthly Reporting

SCHEDULE 6-1
XYZ Corporation
Balance Sheet Detail
Fiscal Year Ending 3/31/___

(continued)

Sample Format for Monthly Reporting (*continued*)

SCHEDULE 6-2
XYZ Corporation
Balance Sheet Detail
September 28, 19__

	Trade Accounts Receivable—Aged from Billing Date					
	0–29 Days	30–59 Days	60–89 Days	Over 90 Days	Total	Delin-quent
This month	$144,535	$29,087	$ 121	$20,129	$193,872	$20,250
Percent	74.55%	15.00%	.06%	10.39%	100%	10.44%
Last month	$138,170	$89,762	$2,269	$25,237	$255,438	$27,506
Percent	54.09%	35.14%	.88%	9.89%	100%	10.76%

ACCOUNTS RECEIVABLE—DAYS OUTSTANDING AND AMOUNTS

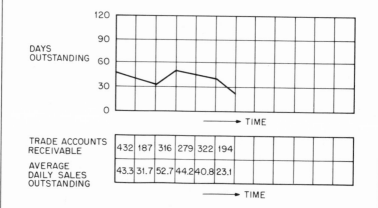

Accounts receivable days outstanding equals (accounts receivable × 360 days) ÷ (revenues for last 3 months × 4).

EXHIBIT 6-2
Sample Format for Monthly Reporting (*continued*)

PROPERTY AND EQUIPMENT

| | Monthly Activity | | | |
Assets	Beginning Balance	Additions	Adjustments	Ending Balance
Land, building, and lease imp's.	$ 61,669	$ 245		$ 61,914
Machinery and equipment	46,407	462		46,869
Furniture and fixtures	28,050	283		28,333
Service equipment	107,958			107,958
Capitalized leases	60,303			60,303
Tooling	20,126	2,412		22,538
Show booth	26,180			26,180
Sign	1,912			1,912
Equipment—Basic Four Co.	130,000			130,000
Accumulated depreciation	(187,107)	(7,480)		(194,587)
Net Fixed Assets	$ 295,498			$ 291,420

SCHEDULE 6-3
XYZ Corporation
Balance Sheet Detail
Fiscal Year Ending 3/31/___

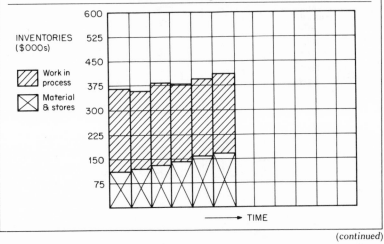

(continued)

EXHIBIT 6-2
Sample Format for Monthly Reporting (*continued*)

BACKLOG

	End Last Month	Orders Received This Month	Sales This Month	End This Month
A	196,885	4,828	74,768	126,945
B	417,851	-0-	120,945	296,906
C	144,245	-0-	-0-	144,245
Total	758,981	4,828	195,713	568,096

EMPLOYEE COUNT

	Actual	Forecast
A	41	32
B	46	47
Total	87	79

SCHEDULE 6-4
XYZ Corporation
Balance Sheet Detail
Fiscal Year Ending 3/31/__

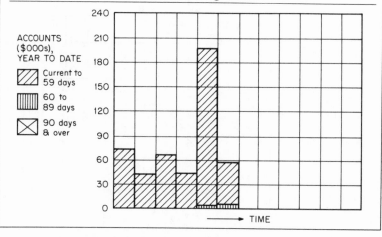

EXHIBIT 6-2
Sample Format for Monthly Reporting (*continued*)

SCHEDULE 6-5
XYZ Corporation
Income Statement Detail
Year Ending 3/31/___

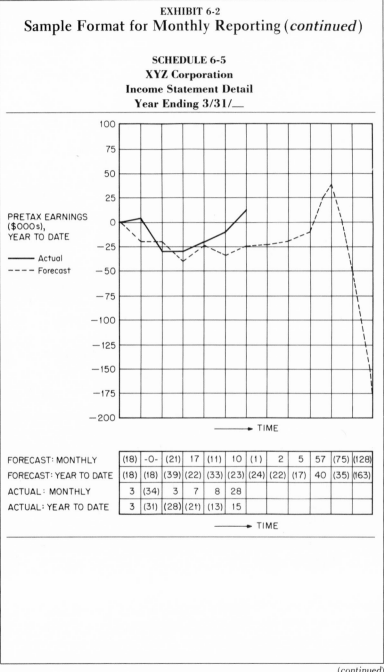

PRETAX EARNINGS
($000s),
YEAR TO DATE

——— Actual
– – – Forecast

———➤ TIME

FORECAST: MONTHLY	(18)	-0-	(21)	17	(11)	10	(1)	2	5	57	(75)	(128)
FORECAST: YEAR TO DATE	(18)	(18)	(39)	(22)	(33)	(23)	(24)	(22)	(17)	40	(35)	(163)
ACTUAL: MONTHLY	3	(34)	3	7	8	28						
ACTUAL: YEAR TO DATE	3	(31)	(28)	(21)	(13)	15						

———➤ TIME

(continued)

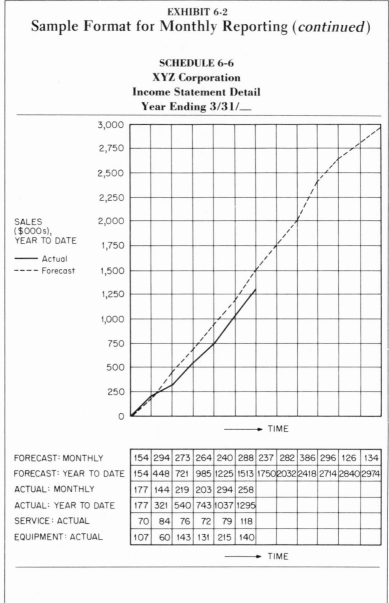

Sample Format for Monthly Reporting (*continued*)

SCHEDULE 6-6
XYZ Corporation
Income Statement Detail
Year Ending 3/31/___

SALES ($000s), YEAR TO DATE
—— Actual
---- Forecast

→ TIME

FORECAST: MONTHLY	154	294	273	264	240	288	237	282	386	296	126	134
FORECAST: YEAR TO DATE	154	448	721	985	1225	1513	1750	2032	2418	2714	2840	2974
ACTUAL: MONTHLY	177	144	219	203	294	258						
ACTUAL: YEAR TO DATE	177	321	540	743	1037	1295						
SERVICE: ACTUAL	70	84	76	72	79	118						
EQUIPMENT: ACTUAL	107	60	143	131	215	140						

→ TIME

EXHIBIT 6-2
Sample Format for Monthly Reporting (*continued*)

SCHEDULE 6-7
XYZ Corporation
Operations Statement Detail
As of _____

	Month		Year to Date	
	Forecast	Actual	Forecast	Actual
Revenue				
Service	104,597	117,732	470,411	500,434
H/O	182,280	120,945	952,460	725,941
Other	-0-	19,772	81,600	69,113
Total Revenue	286,877	258,449	1,504,471	1,295,488
Expenses				
Material cost	43,747	19,309	360,171	195,648
Salaries and wages	119,180	111,762	587,785	531,824
Fringe benefits and P/R taxes	37,755	32,697	176,552	164,555
Training and tuitions	1,600	38	2,600	5,169
Depreciation and amortization	7,750	7,480	44,300	43,449
Repairs and maintenance	3,750	3,650	22,500	19,277
Operating supplies	4,700	6,260	28,200	38,121
Utilities	1,600	2,315	9,600	10,915
Rent—premises	5,200	5,184	29,600	27,922
Rent—equipment	675	772	4,050	3,733
Advertising	3,000	-0-	8,040	5,054
Auto	900	2,086	5,400	7,338
Insurance	1,500	909	9,000	8,094
Relocation expense	-0-	-0-	500	4,672
Outside services	700	1,229	4,200	8,783
Postage	300	617	1,800	2,310
Professional fees	-0-	4,950	7,500	13,133
Taxes and licenses	450	772	2,700	3,372
Telephone	2,700	3,477	16,200	16,844
Travel	7,000	7,820	42,000	42,968
Freight	2,000	1,494	12,000	13,403
Miscellaneous	400	868	7,400	8,273
Interest expense	8,712	8,994	52,512	48,342
Other income	(1,548)	(1,548)	(9,288)	(9,288)
O/H in inventory	—	(6,283)	—	(14,034)
Commissions	4,290	-0-	5,750	7,282
ODC	8,500	420	28,500	16,794
Royalties	11,741	15,080	68,073	56,298
Total expenses	276,602	230,352	1,527,745	1,280,251
Net Income (Loss)	10,275	28,097	(23,274)	15,237

(continued)

The monthly reporting package should go to all key executives for their review. It should be prepared before the tenth day of each month. It is not necessary, in my opinion, to meet and review the package. If a chief executive identifies a problem area, he or she should meet with the appropriate executive and deal directly with the trouble spot. After all, if the right decisions are being made at the weekly cash meetings, the results should be apparent in the monthly summary.

The alarm-reporting system must be tailor-made for each company. It must direct management's attention to the balance sheet, stressing the importance of cash management and assisting in rapid decision making.

Once the company moves out of the crisis, the frequency of the cash planning meetings can be reduced. But let us hope that the lessons learned are not forgotten as business improves!

Chapter 7

Bankruptcy

In the earlier chapters we saw how to survive, establish a new economic base, and move forward. Sometimes, unfortunately, companies wait too long. The key executives or owners look back at the past wearing rose-colored glasses and assuring each other they could not possibly be sailing on the *Titanic*. After all, "we weathered past storms, so we can certainly weather this one." They will fight the daily cash problems and assure their bankers that things will get better soon (hopefully), while a rational analysis would point out to the prudent businessperson that the situation is hopeless. Those who bury their heads in the sand are often surprised when they find themselves caught, unprepared, in an involuntary bankruptcy. If this occurs, there is an excellent chance the company will not survive.

It is, therefore, important to know when the cause is hopeless and when to begin planning for bankruptcy. Many companies have filed for bankruptcy, settled with their creditors, resumed business, and operated successfully. Sometimes, it is possible to settle with creditors on some percentage of current debt or on an informal basis. Creditors will at times accept extended payments, long-term notes, and/or equity positions. The fundamental problem in an informal arrangement is that it is not binding on recalcitrant creditors. It can, however, be carried out successfully if there is a relatively small amount of creditors. This chapter will deal with the more common voluntary filing for relief under the bankruptcy law.

Effective October 1, 1979, Congress repealed the old bankruptcy Act and replaced it with a totally new bankruptcy code. Chapters X, XI, and XII of the old Act are consolidated in Chapter 11 of the new code. The new Chapter 11 does not distinguish between public and private corporations. Statutory criteria are now established to guide the courts in resolving conflicts between the secured creditors and the estate. Under the new law, a debtor cannot force liquidation if creditors do not agree to the debtor's survival plan. Also, a debtor can no longer get creditors to substantially reduce their claims while providing them with limited information about the status of the company. Adequate disclosure is required to solicit acceptance of plans from creditors for both public and private enterprises.

Reorganization under Chapter 11 can be voluntary or involuntary. A company initiates this process by filing a petition with the bankruptcy court. The petitioner may do this without alleging insolvency or the inability to pay debts as they mature.

An involuntary reorganization proceeding is initiated when three or more creditors file a petition with the bankruptcy court or, if there are less than 12 creditors, one creditor may file. Once the involuntary petition is filed, the court, upon request of a party, appoints an interim trustee to operate the business. If a trustee is not appointed, the debtor may continue to operate the business and to use, acquire, and dispose of property in a normal manner. In the involuntary filing, the petitioner must demonstrate cause and could be liable for compensatory and punitive damages if the petition was filed in bad faith.

Creditors will receive notice of the initiation of a bankruptcy proceeding from information provided by the debtor or trustee on a list of creditors, a schedule of assets and liabilities, and a statement of affairs. Creditors and shareholders whose claims are scheduled need not file any proof of claim or interest unless it is listed as "disputed, contingent, or in an amount materially different from that claimed."

After application for relief and the filing of the necessary financial information, the debtor and creditors will begin to devote their energies to the administration of the case. Unsecured creditors could then organize into a creditors' committee, which under the new law is appointed rather than elected. This committee is generally made up of the seven largest creditors who are willing to serve. It is important to note that if, prior to bankruptcy, the unsecured creditors have already created a fairly chosen and representative committee for themselves, then this can be the Chapter 11 committee. Any additional committees of secured creditors or shareholders are appointed. The creditors' committee will hold general meetings of the creditors and, subject to court approval, select accountants, attorneys, and other agents whose fiduciary responsibility is to the creditors as a whole. The committee performs the following major tasks:

1. Recommending whether the business should continue to be operated
2. Recommending whether the court should appoint a trustee or examiner
3. Conducting an investigation of the financial affairs of the debtor
4. Conducting general consultation with the trustee or debtor in the administration of the case
5. Considering the kind of plan it will recommend for the satisfaction of creditors' claims

It is assumed *a priori* that the business will continue to operate unless a court orders otherwise. A party of interest must, therefore, request termination of the business before a judge can decide if a termination is appropriate. Most businesses in a Chapter 11 will undoubtedly continue to have operating losses until a plan is confirmed or the major causes of losses are identified and resolved. If the creditors believe losses can be reduced by a change in management, they may ask the court to appoint a trustee. This is clearly one of the most important decisions the creditors' committee makes in the early stages of a Chapter 11 proceeding. The court *cannot* order the appointment of a trustee on its own initiative.

The filing invokes the *automatic stay* provisions of the bankruptcy law. This gives the debtor the breathing time needed to make key operating decisions.

The debtor is undoubtedly in default on loan agreements and leases, secured creditors probably have begun court action to take possession of their collateral, vendors' credit has probably been curtailed in most cases, and of course the debtor is short or out of cash. In addition, major assets are generally subject to security interests of some kind.

There are times when a creditor seeks relief from the automatic stay by filing a complaint with the court. Under the new law, an enjoined party will be free of the automatic stay unless there is a final trial within 60 days. The burden of proof on the debtor or trustee in such cases is related to the debtor's equity in the property.

In order to give debtors an opportunity to rehabilitate themselves, the bankruptcy proceeding denies secured creditors their contractual right to possession for a period of time. In fact, it allows debtors to "use" some of the collateral for that period of time. The length of time that debtors can use the collateral of the secured creditor is uncertain, subject only to some general guidelines. The key guideline in the determination is that the interest of the secured party in the collateral must be "adequately protected." The secured party cannot dispose of collateral without bankruptcy court approval. If the secured party does not take action, the automatic stay will remain in force until the plan is confirmed or the case dismissed or closed. It must be pointed out that the law distinguishes between *cash* collateral and other forms of collateral.

Cash collateral includes cash, negotiable instruments, and securities; it may not be used without the consent of the secured creditor or until the court authorizes it. Other collateral can be used in the operation of the debtor's business without either the consent of the secured party or the need for a court order. There is in the law a means for the secured creditor to seek relief within 30 days, at a court hearing. The basic philosophy behind the new law seems to be that if "adequate protection" exists, the business will continue to operate, and if it does not, the secured party will reclaim collateral and the business will probably be liquidated.

A debtor operating the business under a Chapter 11 proceeding may obtain unsecured credit. That creditor will have a first priority as an administrative claim. If the business is not being operated, a court order is required. New credit can also be obtained by a lien senior to existing liens, if it can be shown that the interests of the displaced secured creditor is "adequately protected." I suspect this new concept of "adequate protection" will be the focal point of many future disputes.

Debtors and creditors may file a plan of arrangement. If no trustee is appointed, the debtor files a plan during the first 120 days after filing a Chapter 11. Under the old Chapter XI law, only the debtor had the power to file a reorganization plan. Under the new law, which took effect October 1, 1979, once the debtor's exclusive period has ended, stockholders, individual creditors, creditors' committees, or "any party in interest" may also file a plan. This will probably reduce the negotiation leverage that was previously available to the debtor.

In most cases, I suspect debtors will develop the reorganization plan. They will generally segregate creditors into "classes" based on the similarity of their claims. They may also group smaller claims for separate treatment for administrative convenience. Acceptance of creditors sufficient in both number and dollar amount represented is required of each class. Each secured creditor is generally considered a class by itself.

Usually unsecured creditors negotiate whether claims will be satisfied by composition, extension, or the issuance of securities.

A given class of creditors is said to accept a plan of reorganization when of those creditors actually voting, a majority in number and two-thirds in dollar amount represented approve the plan. A class of stockholders (owners) accepts a plan when two-thirds (dollarwise) of those voting accept the plan. Chapter 11 does not necessarily require the approval of all classes of creditors or shareholders. This is because some plans need not affect the rights of certain creditors and owners. In other plans which deal with a given class, that class has no legal financial interest in the reorganized business after applying the appropriate creditor priorities. The acceptance of a given class is not required if its financial interest is not impaired under the plan. While the law provides tests to determine "impairment," this concept too will undoubtedly present some problems in dealing with the rights of creditors and even more complex problems when dealing with the rights of shareholders (owners). An important additional concept is that of "fair and equitable." Even though creditors' and shareholders' interests are impaired, the "class's" acceptance of a reorganization plan is not required if the plan is "fair and equitable" with respect to that class. In general, this occurs either (1) when the class receives the present value of the full amount of its allowed claims, or (2) when it receives whatever reorganization amounts are available after the satisfaction of senior classes, and no junior interest receives any amount in the reorganization plans.

Fundamentally, the new confirmation requirements replace the "best interest" test with the "absolute priority" rules of the past in those cases in which all classes representing impaired claims and interests accept the plan. Under the "best interest" test, even if creditors receive less than full payment, owners may retain their ownership interest providing the creditors receive more than they would on liquidation. This differs from the "absolute priority" rule in that all creditors on a stepwise seniority basis must be provided for in full before owners can retain any interest.

Under the old law, in a Chapter XI case only the debtor could prepetition acceptances of public holders of debt or equity. These solicitations could be included for purposes of confirming the reorganization plan. Now, prior solicitations may be made as long as there is "adequate disclosure" of financial information prior to, and as part of, the solicitations process. The courts can now be flexible in determining what constitutes adequate information. For example, the requirements for audited financial statements, which, because of the time delay, can often doom a proceeding before it starts, can now be waived in light of the quality of the debtor's records and the sophistication of the creditors and security holders. It appears to me that the courts are being given room to study each matter on a case-by-case basis: a situation which should assist debtors, creditors, and equity holders who are operating in good faith. Thus, the court may now approve a debtor's disclosure statement without a valuation of the debtor or an appraisal of the debtor's assets if the court believes such valuation is not necessary to provide adequate information.

The court, of course, must believe that the reorganization is not likely to be followed by a liquidation or a new reorganization proceeding. As in the past, the plan must provide for payment of priority claims, while administrative claims must be paid in cash on the effective date of the plan.

Even priority claim payments have loosened somewhat. Tax claims may now be paid over a six-year period. All other classes of priority claimants may accept by majority vote a deferred cash-payment plan.

In both cases, creditors must receive the present value of their claim. These requirements provide the debtor, in many cases, with substantial relief and, in my experience, often make the difference between failure and survival of the company. The new law is not clear on how to deal with suppliers or others who extend credit during the course of a proceeding.

Another significant reform affirms that confirmation discharges *all* obligations of the debtor to creditors, regardless of whether all obligations are dealt with under the plan or whether those creditors participate in the reorganization. Under the old law, debtors who could not get a discharge in bankruptcy couldn't confirm the plan, and nondischargeable debts survived confirmation.

It appears that the new bankruptcy law eliminates many of the artificial constraints that often prevented the reorganization process from proceeding. Each case is, in fact, different. Everyone loses—debtors, creditors and equity holders, employees, and the community alike—when a company that is economically viable is forced to go out of business.

The reader is encouraged to meet with qualified bankruptcy counsel to understand his or her specific problem. This chapter intends to provide an overall understanding of this important area, but it should not be used for making decisions for a crisis company.

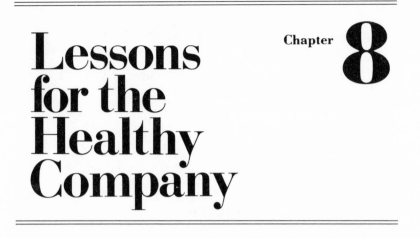

Lessons for the Healthy Company

Chapter **8**

Perhaps your company is doing fine right now. And you'd like to keep it that way. What can you learn from this book? I cannot overemphasize my firsthand observations that most companies in financial difficulty usually have experienced a high level of growth and profits in the years preceding their downslide. Suddenly, something goes wrong. Careful study of the earlier chapters can provide meaningful lessons for the healthy company. A complete list of what can go wrong would fill an entire text. However, I would like to identify some of the more important lessons:

- Maintain appropriate contact with your existing financial institutions, key vendors, key management personnel, alternative sources of financing, and shareholders.
- Maintain and update the corporate strategy annually and include a contingency plan.
- Be sure that your reporting system includes good balance sheet management in addition to profit and loss types of reports. Evaluate frequency of reporting. This includes cash management and asset control.
- Find, engage, and maintain effective relationships with attorneys, accountants, and consultants.

153

While the company is in good health:

- Keep a few "street fighters" in your employ and as a part of your advisory team.
- Understand bankruptcy law.
- Set and maintain personal goals at least annually.
- Give your company an annual health exam.

MAINTAIN CONTACT WITH THOSE WHOSE HELP YOU MAY NEED SOMEDAY

When your company is prospering, banks are happy with you, vendors can't do enough for you, personnel are content, and you are the "darling" of the shareholders. Under these circumstances, it often appears unnecessary to "waste time" meeting with financial institutions, key vendors, and crucial employees. Establishing an on-going dialogue with shareholders is less appealing than boasting about how great the business is today and how much better it will be tomorrow.

Executives of a healthy company would be better advised to maintain contact with their existing financial institutions at the highest level. The president or chief operating officer of the company should know an equally high level banker, while the chief financial officer should maintain contact at the branch manager level. Breakfasts or lunches provide a congenial setting to get to know each other, develop trust and confidence, and keep each other informed of current state of affairs. At these meetings you can learn the career goals of your banker, how bank decisions are made, the role of the loan committee, and the extent of his or her influence and authority. It is also an opportunity to familiarize your banker with the details of your business and introduce your key management people in a positive environment. Get into a position where you are on a first-name basis and can get on the phone to expedite decisions when necessary.

While this is all happening, make it a point to keep in contact with other financial institutions. Whenever possible, spread some of the business around. Consider keeping your personal business in a different institution. Become familiar with other sources of funding, know who their key people are, and be on the lookout for every opportunity to meet them. These other contacts will improve your leverage with your existing financial institutions during good times and are absolutely imperative should you fall "out of favor" with your banker.

Each of your key vendors also has a president—a human body who wants to know you better when you are a good customer. Get to know these presidents on a first-name basis. Develop mutual feelings of respect and trust with them. Do this before you come eyeball to eyeball with their credit manager, who may threaten to stop shipment of critical products unless you send prompt payment.

Employee loyalty is considered a luxury when times are good. After all, you have an attractive, profitable company. If certain employees do not meet your requirements, they can be replaced easily! Often key executives of a successful company feel they can do no wrong and are intolerant of adverse criticism. They forget to listen, to care, and to see their employees as people who can think for themselves and have worthwhile suggestions and personal problems. It is during these healthy periods that listening, helping, and doing favors can go a long way to create a sense of loyalty. When the chips are down and you need long hours of work at reduced pay, you may need to call upon that loyalty. An insufficient number of loyal employees is often the Achilles' heel of a problem company. If a company in crisis experiences a mass exodus of its key people, it will surely fail, because it is incapable of functioning.

MAINTAIN AND UPDATE THE CORPORATE STRATEGY

Think how much easier it would be to face a crisis if your company already had worked out a strategy. Imagine further that the strategy also included a contingency plan to handle the possibility of a pessimistic year. While we all hope that the contingency plan will be unnecessary, at the first sign of a down turn, your company can begin to activate the plan. My experience is that one of the greatest causes of failure in overcoming a crisis is the inability of management to respond promptly. Acknowledgment of the crisis, unfortunately, is the starting point for *planning* in many companies. In fact, that recognition should trigger *implementation* of the plan.

Strategy and contingency plans should be worked out in sufficient detail so that each key manager knows his or her role well in advance.

EMPHASIZE BALANCE SHEET REPORTING

Most executives in business have been trained to read profit and loss and related information. This includes fixed and variable budgets, responsibility reporting, and profit-center accounting. The balance sheet and related analysis, considered to be less important, have been virtually ignored. This deficiency is a serious mistake. I would prefer an executive to visualize a business as a succession of balance sheets. The profit and loss statement is merely a way of explaining the changes between periods. Through excess investment in capital expansion utilizing short-term funds, the executive can be lulled into thinking that all is well. Although it appears that profits are good and growth is strong, the cash position may be eroding to a point of no return. Current assets may seem high, but if inventory levels are too high and are composed of slow-moving, obsolete products, inventory value is less than may be recorded in the accounting records. An accrual accounting of expenses and revenues can also be deceptive. Cash disbursements for items that cannot be expensed still reduce the cash balance. Slow accounts receivable and aged inventory still tie up cash, even though profits look acceptable. How many executives look at the structuring of debt and equity before a financial problem arises?

To be forewarned is to be forearmed. Study and understand the balance sheet. At a minimum, there should be reports on cash flow, source and use of funds, detailed accounts receivable, accounts payable, inventory analysis accompanied by a tight control over existing capital assets, and proposed capital outlays.

MAINTAIN APPROPRIATE PROFESSIONAL RELATIONSHIPS

To avoid the "vultures" when the crisis occurs, you must seek out their counterparts, the "professionals." These are accountants, attorneys, and consultants who are experienced, competent, and trustworthy. They will give you the independent kind of advice only outsiders can provide. They must, however, be familiar with your business. Rushing them in at the last minute to solve a crisis is often not workable, particularly if your business is at all complicated.

My advice is to establish relationships with such professionals now. Use them on a limited basis to improve your company and deal with its problems. In this way, a mutual trust will develop. The professionals will have a loyalty to you which can be called upon during the crisis.

KEEP SOME "STREET FIGHTERS"

When business is going well, it creates a good impression if all of your key people are sophisticated Ivy League types. The carpeting gets a bit thicker, the offices a little larger, the desks fancier, and the insulation from reality unbearable. Sometimes the insulation between the executive offices and the "working troops" is so thick that obvious danger signs are ignored.

Therefore, I urge you, dear reader, to keep the eyeshaded controller, that swearing production manager, that unrelentless expeditor, in your employ. These hard-boiled individuals may be a little hard to handle when the sun is shining, but you will cry out for them when the rains begin. These tough, tenacious people may prove to be a major asset when impossible tasks have to be accomplished in short periods of time.

UNDERSTAND BANKRUPTCY LAW

Reread the chapter on bankruptcy law. Find out who the best counsels in town are. Meet with them and make certain you have structured your company and your personal affairs with full consideration to these laws. Careful attention to this area could be worth a great deal. Bankruptcy law is a specialized field. Your general counsel will generally not be qualified to advise you in this sphere.

SET AND MAINTAIN PERSONAL GOALS

I always recommend that each year my clients write, in order of importance, his or her major "personal" goals on 3 × 5 inch cards. On the back of each card the client is asked to spell out as clearly as possible the plan to be followed in achieving these goals. The goals should be read each day and updated whenever priorities are changed, goals are achieved, or a card is no longer relevant. Do not show the cards to anyone. If you know that someone else will read them, you tend to be a bit dishonest in order to appear unselfish.

Now, compare these goals with the goals set for your company to make certain you have not set yourself on the "anxiety" path. For example, you may want to spend more time with your wife and children at home, but have a corporate goal to diversify geographically. The latter aspiration involves extensive travel. Something must give. If you don't want it to be your heart, then you must deal with this dichotomy at the onset. Why, you ask, is this important to a company in crisis? Business failures occur on a daily basis in this country because executives, out of their own anxiety, become ineffective, allowing the roof to cave in around them. In my experience, an important buttress against the onset of an anxiety attack is an executive who is clear about who he or she is and what he or she wants out of life.

GIVE YOUR COMPANY AN ANNUAL HEALTH CHECK

Most of us would agree that some sort of periodic health check is important for us and our loved ones. We willingly submit to blood-pressure tests, x-rays, urinating into thimble-sized cups, and having our skin punctured in search of blood. We feel a lot better when the doctor subsequently informs us that we are in good health. If a problem is spotted in the early stages, the chances are excellent for a good prognosis. Under any conditions, the results of an exam provide a base set of data with which to measure changes and patterns that could create problems in the future.

Executives of living, breathing companies rarely, however, take the same annual health check for the entity they direct. They feel it would be too costly, too disturbing. They would rather rely on gut feelings. They don't believe in preventive medicine as it applies to their company.

It is my advice that a company evaluate its health annually. The major areas of the business should be assigned values of relative importance. Each area should be carefully reviewed.

Your business is a conglomeration of money, material, and human activity awaiting proper direction. You are managing these resources. With the proper lead time, replace and modify these resources to fit the needs of the marketplace. Up-and-down business cycles are a way of life in our economy. To operate by the seat of your pants is to increase the probability that you will lose your pants completely.

Exhibit 8-1 is a sample questionnaire to assist a company in carrying out such a checkup. This type of analysis can be converted into a point-scoring system which identifies ranges of excellent, good, fair, and poor health.

EXHIBIT 8-1
Health Check Questionnaire

I. ORGANIZATION

1. Obtain a detailed organization chart from top management. Also develop a "bottoms up" informal chart. Understand and explain the differences. Review any major organizational structure changes in the past three years.
2. Prepare detailed job descriptions for each executive, showing:
   a. General function and title
   b. Responsibilities
   c. Authority
   d. Reporting relationship
3. How frequently are formal meetings held between executives? What areas are generally discussed? Are they generally meetings involving decisions?
4. Is there a policy and procedures manual? Who is responsible for its maintenance?
5. What is the composition of the board? How many are officers of the company? Do any consult for the company? Any relatives? What are the fee arrangements? How often do they meet? What is their role?
6. Is there adequate management? How is each key executive compensated? Compare:
   a. Cars and expenses
   b. Options and stock
   c. Base salary
   d. Bonus
   e. Other incentives
7. Review each of these basic trouble areas:
   a. Too wide a span of control
   b. Too many management levels
   c. Inconsistent compensation
   d. Duplication of work or responsibility
   e. Vacuum of responsibility
   f. Dual reporting
   g. Differing objectives in the same group
   h. No backup for key personnel
   i. Responsibilities not matching authority
8. Summarize staffing levels for each department. Are the levels proper?
9. How does the company recruit and train personnel? How are people selected for promotion? Is lateral as well as vertical movement allowed? Are future executives being developed? Who is responsible? Is promotion from outside or from within?

EXHIBIT 8-1
Health Check Questionnaire (*continued*)

10. Has top management under- or overdelegated functions? Are they in control of the company? Is there any unhealthy conflict?
11. How well are the three major functions of the organization being carried out?
    a. *Planning:* long-range plans, short-range plans, forecasts, budgets, new products, recapitalization, expansion, restructurings, etc.
    b. *Operation:* procedures, controls, standards, forms and documents, approval authority
    c. *Control:* accounting policies and procedures, good financial information, internal audit
12. How frequently is performance evaluated? What is the method? Who does the evaluation? How are the results reported and filed?
13. Is there excessive reporting, memos, etc.?
14. Does the company place undue emphasis on one function and insufficient emphasis on other functions?
15. To what extent are committees used? How do they communicate and coordinate? Who do they report to?
16. Is the organization structure functional or territorial by product, by customer classification, etc.? Is there conflict between central and local functions?
17. Describe the line and staff relationships within the organization. What is the real staff authority? Is there great confusion between functional and line authority?
18. Has the company considered the economics of purchased versus owned services?
19. Consider the organization as a whole in relation to the fundamental principles of:
    a. Unity of objective
    b. Efficiency
    c. Span of management
    d. Division of work
    e. Functional definition
    f. The scalar principle
    g. The exception principle
    h. Unity of command
    i. Unity of direction
    j. Flexibility

II. FINANCE, ACCOUNTING, AND MANAGEMENT REPORTING

Bank Relations

1. Is the company basically on solid financial footing?
2. Who is the company contact with the banks? At what level in the

(continued)

EXHIBIT 8-1
Health Check Questionnaire (*continued*)

organization is the bank representative? How often do they meet? Do they get along?

3. What reports are submitted to the bank? How frequently?
4. Is the company line of credit adequate? How was the amount of the line determined? Is there a good history of paying back debt? Have any loan requests been recently turned down?
5. Review any presentations made to the bank in the past 12 months.
6. Review any loan agreements. Note ratio requirements, causes of default, and restrictions.
7. Is there any current pressure to pay down the loan? Has the company considered these approaches to increasing cash?
   a. Maximizing bank float
   b. Accelerating receivable collection and factoring
   c. Stretching vendor payments
   d. Selling idle assets
   e. Selling certain inventories
   f. Refinancing or selling certain real estate
   g. Establishing across-the-board cost reductions
   h. Idling certain facilities
   i. Eliminating certain service departments
8. How highly leveraged is the company? What is the current debt/ equity ratio?
9. Is there any long-term debt? Describe.
10. Is there any intercompany financing?
11. What is the company's D&B rating?
12. Review its long-term financing plans.

Accounting

1. Obtain an organization and staffing chart of the accounting function showing the various line and staff relations.
2. Who is the outside auditor? Review 10K's or annual reports for the past three years. Do horizontal and vertical analysis. Does the company have unqualified opinions?
3. Is the chart of accounts adequate?
4. Is there a complete accounting manual showing policies, systems, and procedures?
5. Review the mechanics of the cost accounting system. Does it make sense? Are, in fact, all the actual costs captured, or does the system rely excessively on estimates?
6. Is the system automated? If so, what equipment is being utilized? Evaluate.
7. Review the flow of paperwork into the accounting department.

EXHIBIT 8-1
Health Check Questionnaire (*continued*)

Review systems and procedures within the department. Obtain all forms and documents.

8. What is the company's policy in the establishment of reserves? How do they deal with certain contingent liabilities? Is the company properly reserved?
9. Review the basis for valuing inventories, receivables, investments, and fixed assets.
10. Review any differences, if any, between the book and tax basis of accounting.
11. Is there a formal record-retention and form-control program?
12. Are the financial reports prepared in a timely manner? Do copies go to the right people? Are the reports all being used? Is the frequency correct? Are the reports cumbersome?

Budgets and Reporting

1. Are budgets prepared and approved by the board of directors?
2. Who is responsible for budget preparation?
3. Are actual costs reported against the budget? Is this information provided to officers? To the board?
4. Is the concept of responsibility reporting being utilized?
5. What methods does the company use to forecast sales and to estimate expenses? Is there a formalized procedure? Are they developed from the top down or from the bottom up?
6. Are responsible officers and managers required to report significant deviations from the budgeted values?
7. Is there effective authorization and control over expenditures?
8. Is there a budget for capital expenditures?
9. Is the business departmentalized for reporting purposes?
10. Do monthly financial reports follow the organization structure?
11. Is there any cash management system? Control over the balance sheet?
12. Does the company have a complete profit planning system?
13. Does the budget system cover all areas? Or are there vacuums of control?
14. Does the top executive believe in the system and use it?
15. How good are the actual costs that are being compared to the budget? Are they directly collected at the same level of detail as the budget? Are controllable and noncontrollable costs segregated by area of responsibility?
16. Does the company properly measure the financial performance of each of its profit centers?

(*continued*)

EXHIBIT 8-1
Health Check Questionnaire (*continued*)

III. MARKETING AND SALES

1. Indicate the following for each of the principal products or product lines manufactured or purchased for resale by the company over the past five years:
   a. Dollar and unit sales by major product line.
   b. Principal competitors. How is the market divided?
   c. Share of market by product line versus competitors.
   d. The gross profit margins.
   e. Method of selling.
2. Schedule sales by product line for the next five years. Show how scheduled marketing, selling, and distribution costs compare with capacity.
3. Study the principal customers.
   a. Rank by volume and name
   b. Rank by type of industry
   c. Rank by geographical location
   d. Analyze stability of customers for past five years
4. Does the company utilize market research?
   a. Surveys and questionnaires
   b. Collection of key statistics
   c. Test marketing
5. How does the company evaluate new products? What approvals are required? How are the programs initiated and approved? How is the capital investment evaluated?
6. What are the costs of marketing, and how does this compare to averages in the industry? Obtain staffing levels and full job descriptions for all personnel involved in the function. Show how marketing relates to the rest of the organization.
7. Does the company have a marketing plan? If so, how frequently is the plan updated?
8. Show the volume of products marketed through:
   a. The company's sales department
   b. Franchised dealers or agents
   c. Brokers
   d. Direct mail
   e. Company and facilities
   f. Other
9. Describe for item 8 above the franchise agreements and the method of compensating distributors.
10. What are the sales territories and how were they developed?

EXHIBIT 8-1
Health Check Questionnaire (*continued*)

11. Construct the sales organization, staffing levels, responsibilities, and related methods of compensation.
12. What material is provided to the salespeople to familiarize them with the company and product and to teach them how to sell?
13. Are the key executives guilty of these common marketing mistakes?
    a. Overestimating the share of market, brand-name identification, standing in the trade
    b. Overestimating price resistance
    c. Underestimating the strength of the competition
    d. Placing too much reliance on personal observations only
    e. Oversimplifying data; being unwilling to dig in and study
14. How does the company deal with the quality-price relationship? Price-volume relationship?
15. Show the steps taken by the company to establish pricing for new and for existing products. How are prices updated? Who decides, and what input data is used to make the decision?
    a. How are discounts considered?
    b. How are marketing, selling, and distribution costs related to gross profit?
    c. Are prices competitive?
    d. How are the engineering, research, and manufacturing costs estimated?
16. What is the relationship between sales and marketing?
17. Does the company have a sales manual and clear sales policies? Does the company thoroughly understand the pricing and sales policies of its competitors? Is source data for this obtained from the sales and marketing department, customers, industry publications, etc.?
18. What kinds of sales analysis reports are available? Does the company know:
    a. Weak and strong territories?
    b. Performance by product, area, and salesperson?
    c. Distribution of product by area?
    d. Trend and market position by sales area?
    e. Sales expenses related to territories?
19. What is the company's approach toward the hiring and training of sales personnel?
20. Is the sales organization too spread out? How good is the daily control over the salespeople?
21. Who controls the advertising decisions? Obtain the advertising budget for the coming years. What is the basis for establishing advertising costs?

(continued)

EXHIBIT 8-1
Health Check Questionnaire (*continued*)

22. How is advertising allocated to the various media?
    a. Newspapers
    b. Radio
    c. National magazines
    d. Outdoor posters
    e. Television
    f. Point of purchase
    g. Other
    Is the appropriate media being selected to meet the company's objectives?
23. Does the firm utilize an advertising agency? If so:
    a. Who in the company works with the agency?
    b. Who in the agency is responsible for the company's account?
    c. Get specific examples of contributions made by the agency.
    d. What are the fee arrangements?
    e. How much time does the agency spend in the field with both salespeople and customers?
24. Generally evaluate the company against some of these basic marketing- and sales-related causes for business failures:
    a. Unrealistic pricing and discount policy
    b. Poor incentives for salespeople, wholesalers, distributors
    c. Product obsolescence
    d. Inadequate sales promotion
    e. Advertising directed to a declining age group
    f. Quality not matching advertising claims
    g. Failure to modernize either product or package
    h. Selling costs out of control
25. How does the company organize for good customer relations?
    a. What is the place of customer relations in the company?
    b. What does the customer relations executive or adviser do?
    c. Is there a public relations policy?
    d. Are all these policies effectively communicated to the employee?
    e. Is there a good record of customer turnover and a file summarizing why customers have left? Is the file ever used to make marketing and sales decisions?
    f. Does the company know its customer profile?
    g. Do these programs have the support of top management, and is there an adequate follow-up?
26. How does the company deal with:
    a. Stockholder relations?
    b. Dealer relations?
    c. Creditor relations?

EXHIBIT 8-1
Health Check Questionnaire (*continued*)

27. Is business seasonal? Has management considered anticyclical products?

IV. DISTRIBUTION

1. How is the distribution function organized? Is it part of the sales or operating segment of the company or is it an independent function? Consider staffing levels.
2. How does the company keep track of its distribution costs (by territory, product line, etc.)?
3. List the modes of distribution by appropriate categories:
   a. Truck
   b. Direct transport
   c. Train
   d. Boat
   e. Plane
4. Describe the physical distribution system, including:
   a. Storage
   b. Inventory control
   c. Order entry—small versus large orders
   d. Billing
   e. Receiving
   f. Shipping
   g. Transportation
5. Chart out the paperwork flow related to item 4 above.
6. Review flow of materials, analyze space assignment and utilization, study material handling and storage equipment, and evaluate stock location and picking systems.
7. Review the finished goods inventory management system:
   a. Chart the required information flow
   b. Define record keeping procedures
   c. Review methods of forecasting
   d. Review reorder rules and the establishment of inventory levels
   e. Review warehouse replenishment methods and procedures
   f. Review the order entry system
   g. Evaluate the inventory reporting system
8. Does the distribution system accomplish:
   a. Good customer service?
   b. Low cost?
   c. Minimal inventory levels?
   Does the company attempt to relate these elements?

(continued)

EXHIBIT 8-1
Health Check Questionnaire (*continued*)

9. How are products moved to the ultimate consumer? Is this the best way?
   a. Direct from plant
   b. From company warehouses
   c. From public warehouses
   d. Through company-owned retail outlets
   e. Through independent retail outlets
   f. From jobbers' warehouses
10. Are warehouses properly located? Are there too many or too few? Are they too large or too small?

V. MANUFACTURING

Material Control

1. Does the company have up-to-date bills of material? How is the bill used by engineering, purchasing, and manufacturing? Who controls the bill of material?
2. Are route sheets used to move the material between departments?
3. How are perpetual raw material and in-process inventory records maintained?
4. If possible, get an ABC evaluation of purchased parts, including prices, availability, and obsolescence.
5. Review the entire purchasing system. What triggers an order, and how is the quantity to be ordered determined? Is some type of EOQ system in force? How does purchasing tie in with production control? Who does purchasing report to in the organization?
6. Obtain staffing and job description data from the purchasing department.
7. How are the material standards established? Who uses them? How frequently are they updated?
8. Is the flow of material in control from ordering (and through receiving, issuing to line, and in-process control) to finished goods?
9. Are the inventory adjustments between physical and book generally significant? What were they for the last three audits?
10. Is there a written purchasing policy? Are vendor bids required for new materials? Are there approval levels? How good is the internal control?
11. Are products delivered on time to distribution? Is there good customer service? Is there accurate delivery quoting? Are there frequent stockouts?
12. How does the company evaluate and make a key decision?

EXHIBIT 8-1
Health Check Questionnaire (*continued*)

13. Review the physical inventory system:
    a. Stock location and stock-picking methods
    b. Adequate space
    c. Smooth flow and control of materials
14. In moving materials, are modern material-handling devices being employed (conveyor, lift trucks, etc.)? Has the company considered:
    a. Use of engineering economy principles in selecting equipment and methods?
    b. Maximizing size of unit handled?
    c. Reducing the ratio of dead weight of equipment to the live weight of load?
    d. Employing effective preventative maintenance?
    e. Minimizing distance of material movement and maximizing use of gravity?
15. Review entire inventory control system, including:
    a. Inventory analysis (cost-usage, weeks on hand)
    b. Classification for selective controls
    c. Order quantities, reorder points, and safety stock levels
    d. Inventory reporting system

Labor Control

1. What are the major characteristics of the work force?
    a. Number (by seasons, if necessary)
    b. Union, nonunion
    c. Skilled, unskilled
    d. Sex, age
    e. Direct versus indirect
    f. Wage rates (hourly, weekly, monthly, etc.)
    g. Turnover rate by classification
2. Show the major features and obtain the underlying documents of any pay plans:
    a. Union-related
    b. Incentive systems
    c. Stock options, profit sharing
    d. Holiday and overtime
    e. Personnel manual, if available
    f. Guarantees
    g. Fringe benefits
    Is the overall compensation package competitive with other companies in the industry?
3. Summarize the union-management history over the past five years.

(continued)

EXHIBIT 8-1
Health Check Questionnaire (*continued*)

4. How are labor standards established? Who uses them? How frequently are they updated? Are work measurement techniques used in their development (work sampling, time studies, predetermined standards, etc.)?

5. What kind of labor reporting exists? How is labor performance measured?

6. Are individual work stations well laid out?

7. Review the current production scheduling system. Are the lines properly balanced?

8. Have all pension programs been reviewed in the light of recent federal legislation?

9. Obtain staffing levels and activity indicators for each production department.

10. How is the QC function related to production performance?

11. Are these types of functions being filled by the company?
    a. Director of personnel
    b. Public relations
    c. Wage and salary administration
    d. Labor relations
    e. Medical, safety, training, counselling

12. How are employees hired, promoted, and terminated? What are the related forms, interviews, and tests?

13. Is there a formal evaluation system utilized as a basis for compensation?

14. Are there any employee suggestion systems?

15. Are the employee relations policies formalized?
    a. Employment practices
    b. Training and development
    c. Collective bargaining
    d. Wages (job evaluation, job rating, etc.)
    e. Hours (overtime, holidays, down time, etc.)
    f. Working conditions
    g. Grievances
    h. Insurance, services, legal aid
    i. Lunch hour, cafeteria
    j. Savings, stock ownership, housing
    k. Discipline

16. Review the employment records.

17. If the company has a multiplant operation, are the labor policies consistent? Are they in keeping with local practices?

18. How good are employee communications and morale, between levels of line management (above and below)?

EXHIBIT 8-1
Health Check Questionnaire (*continued*)

Overhead Control

1. List the various overhead accounts and the costs that they include. Are there overhead budgets? Is the budget static or flexible?
2. Separate the fixed, variable, and semivariable costs, and establish the break-even points for the company.
3. Is there a clear separation between manufacturing overhead and general and administrative and selling expenses?
4. List all the overhead departments. Obtain the staffing levels and the appropriate organization charts. How are overhead expenses related to product costs? Is the method of allocation of cost appropriate? Do overhead expenses appear too high?
5. Have standards been set up for indirect labor, maintenance, and other services? How is the performance of these functions measured (mechanical, electrical, janitorial, etc.)?
6. How are general overhead costs, such as depreciation, engineering, taxes, and insurance, evaluated?
7. Review the layout of all facilities and analyze:
   a. Layout and space utilization
   b. Material flow
   c. Balance between work centers
   d. Adjacency requirements
   e. Capacity considerations and expansion alternatives
   f. Equipment appraisal and utilization
8. Obtain location, square footage, and capital investment data for all operating locations. Comment on number, size, and geographical distribution. Is there excess or inadequate plant capacity?
9. How are new capital investments evaluated?
10. Determine if lines are properly balanced.
11. In general, is the manufacturing operation currently efficient, and are there adequate programs to meet future requirements?
12. What is the quality of communication between manufacturing and the sales, marketing, and finance functions?

VI. OFFICER LEGAL EXPOSURES

1. Does the company check some of these common ways that fraud is committed?
   a. Lapping
   b. Checks to fictitious payees
   c. Legitimate checks with forged endorsements

(continued)

EXHIBIT 8-1
Health Check Questionnaire (*continued*)

    d. Fictitious payroll checks
    e. Misappropriated cash received by mail
    f. Items ordered for the company and diverted for personal gain
    g. Special prices to vendors for kickbacks
    h. Understated or overstated entries to general or subsidiary ledger from books of original entry
    i. Inventory items taken and proceeds misappropriated from sale of funds

2. Does the company have an annual internal control audit?
3. Is there an internal audit function? If so, who does it report to?
4. Does the company employ these basic methods to combat fraud?
    a. Careful employee selection and training
    b. Proper supervision
    c. Forced vacations
    d. Adequate pay
    e. Knowledge of family problems and living habits
    f. Bonding or insurance
    g. Comparative financial statements and financial ratios
    h. Audited internal check
5. Does the company have D&O coverage? If so, what is the nature of the coverage?
6. Are there any loans or major advances to corporate officers and directors?
7. Do any officers or directors have any business interests adverse to the corporation?
8. Has the corporation recently entered into any extraneous lines of business?
9. Does the board meet at least monthly, and do they receive a complete financial package?
10. Are all officers aware of insider short swing profit rules?
11. Are there any acquisitions, sales, or transfers resulting in a loss of corporate assets?
12. Is there poor attendance at directors' meetings? Infrequent meetings? How good is the documentation?
13. Are there adequate checks on reporting to SEC (8K, etc.) and on appropriateness of press releases?
14. Are there any inappropriate corporate gifts or contributions?
15. Are officers and directors given adequate time to review reports and documents before signing? Is all material information disclosed?
16. Are there any cases of excessive compensation?
17. Are favorable as well as unfavorable facts promptly publicized?

EXHIBIT 8-1
Health Check Questionnaire (*continued*)

18. Is the corporation qualified to do business, and does it have the proper licenses in the states in which it is doing business?
19. Have there been any improper purchases of stock?
20. Have there been any insider leaks?
21. Has there been any dissolution of a substantial portion of the company's assets?
22. Is there a policy to relocate and rotate key personnel?

Index

to r
effec.
niques
e is hop.
bankrupt

ou how to
fronted
will disco
—the sigr
w to use it
ne the lon
t you can do
d to *keep* it
de:

company in

isting fears,
ng the gen-